AF784690

CONTENTS

THE HEALTH CARE CHOICE ACT

TUESDAY, JUNE 28, 2005

HOUSE OF REPRESENTATIVES,
COMMITTEE ON ENERGY AND COMMERCE,
SUBCOMMITTEE ON HEALTH,
Washington, DC.

The subcommittee met, pursuant to notice, at 10:05 a.m., in room 2123, Rayburn House Office Building, Hon. Nathan Deal (chairman) presiding.

Members present: Representatives Deal, Hall, Gillmor, Norwood, Cubin, Shimkus, Shadegg, Buyer, Myrick, Burgess, Barton (ex officio), Brown, Waxman, Pallone, Eshoo, Green, Baldwin, and Dingell (ex officio).

Staff present: Chuck Clapton, chief health counsel; Bill O'Brien, legislative analyst; Eugenia Edwards, legislative clerk; Brandon Clark, Health policy coordinator; Bridgett Taylor, minority professional staff; Amy Hall, minority professional staff; and Jessica McNiece, minority research assistant.

Mr. DEAL. Good morning. I will call this hearing to order and welcome everyone here.

We are pleased to have such a distinguished panel before us, and we look forward to hearing your testimony soon. If I talk fast enough and the other members talk fast enough, we will get to your testimony rather soon. But first of all, we have opening statements.

Today, the subcommittee is here to examine H.R. 2355, the Health Care Choice Act of 2005. I want to thank Congressman Shadegg and his staff for their hard work, their cooperation, and their willingness to make some modifications to this initial legislation to accommodate some of the issues that we will hear raised, I think, even today.

I commend you, Mr. Shadegg, and your staff for your hard work on this issue.

I would also like to thank our panel of witnesses for appearing before us. We know that any time you take time out of your schedules to be here that it is an inconvenience, but you have points of view that we do wish to hear from, and we appreciate your sharing those with us.

But the reason we are here today is that we are told that sometime during this past year 45 million Americans, approximately, were without health insurance. For most of us, we think this is an unacceptable number.

Today, we are here to explore one suggestion as to an innovative way to try to reduce that number of uninsured. Of course, covering the uninsured is a complex issue, and probably no one simple answer is going to solve all the problems. It requires complex solutions as well. Perhaps today is a step in the right direction for finding some of those solutions.

Again, I thank my colleagues for their work on this issue, and I know that there has been a cooperative effort within this subcommittee.

With that, I will conclude my opening statement and call on my good friend, Mr. Brown, the ranking member, for his opening statement.

Mr. BROWN. Thank you, Mr. Chairman.

And thank you to our witnesses for joining us, especially the insurance commissioner, Mike Kreidler, who was a member of, not this subcommittee, but the full committee back several Congresses ago. So, good to see all of you—especially you, Mike—thanks for coming.

I want to thank Mr. Shadegg for contributing to the insurance debate. Although I cannot support the proposal he offers, we should commend him for focusing on this important issue.

I see three basic arguments for this legislation, and I want to go through them one at a time. One, consumers need more choice, they should be able to pick the health plan that is best for them. This bill doesn't give consumers more choice, it gives certain consumers more choice, the ones who are in perfect health. As far as for the consumers who don't have a clean bill of health, maybe they can get on the waiting list for their State's high-risk pool if their State has one.

When you let insurers snake out from under consumer protections, like guaranteed issue, coverage may be less expensive for some people; that is because it isn't available at all to others. The whole notion of choice is anathema to the basic idea of insurance.

When high-risk consumers can pick the health insurance that is best for them, it is called adverse selection. The plans that attract a bigger share of high-risk employees—of high-risk enrollees simply go out of business.

When relatively low-risk enrollees can pick the insurance that is best for them, it is called favorable selection. Health plans that attract a bigger share of low-risk enrollees aren't really insurers; they are more like bookies, the odds are always in their favor.

Adverse selection destabilizes insurance markets and leaves the people most in need of coverage without coverage. The second premise is that it is burdensome for health insurers to comply with 50 different sets of regulations.

I have no doubt that is burdensome. There is always a tradeoff between Federal and State regulation. But does that mean insurers should be able to canvass the 50 States, choose which set of regulations they like best, and comply only with those?

H.R. 2355 doesn't enhance flexibility, it makes the lowest State standard the de facto national standard. The third premise is that benefit mandates are bad because they make every enrollee pay for services that only a few people need. Insurance itself makes every enrollee pay for services that only a few people need. So let us talk about those evil benefit mandates.

THE HEALTH CARE CHOICE ACT

HEARING

BEFORE THE

SUBCOMMITTEE ON HEALTH

OF THE

COMMITTEE ON ENERGY AND COMMERCE

HOUSE OF REPRESENTATIVES

ONE HUNDRED NINTH CONGRESS

FIRST SESSION

ON

H.R. 2335

JUNE 28, 2005

Serial No. 109–23

Printed for the use of the Committee on Energy and Commerce

Available via the World Wide Web: http://www.access.gpo.gov/congress/house

U.S. GOVERNMENT PRINTING OFFICE

22–986PDF WASHINGTON : 2005

For sale by the Superintendent of Documents, U.S. Government Printing Office
Internet: bookstore.gpo.gov Phone: toll free (866) 512–1800; DC area (202) 512–1800
Fax: (202) 512–2250 Mail: Stop SSOP, Washington, DC 20402–0001

COMMITTEE ON ENERGY AND COMMERCE

JOE BARTON, Texas, *Chairman*

RALPH M. HALL, Texas
MICHAEL BILIRAKIS, Florida
Vice Chairman
FRED UPTON, Michigan
CLIFF STEARNS, Florida
PAUL E. GILLMOR, Ohio
NATHAN DEAL, Georgia
ED WHITFIELD, Kentucky
CHARLIE NORWOOD, Georgia
BARBARA CUBIN, Wyoming
JOHN SHIMKUS, Illinois
HEATHER WILSON, New Mexico
JOHN B. SHADEGG, Arizona
CHARLES W. "CHIP" PICKERING, Mississippi, *Vice Chairman*
VITO FOSSELLA, New York
ROY BLUNT, Missouri
STEVE BUYER, Indiana
GEORGE RADANOVICH, California
CHARLES F. BASS, New Hampshire
JOSEPH R. PITTS, Pennsylvania
MARY BONO, California
GREG WALDEN, Oregon
LEE TERRY, Nebraska
MIKE FERGUSON, New Jersey
MIKE ROGERS, Michigan
C.L. "BUTCH" OTTER, Idaho
SUE MYRICK, North Carolina
JOHN SULLIVAN, Oklahoma
TIM MURPHY, Pennsylvania
MICHAEL C. BURGESS, Texas
MARSHA BLACKBURN, Tennessee

JOHN D. DINGELL, Michigan
Ranking Member
HENRY A. WAXMAN, California
EDWARD J. MARKEY, Massachusetts
RICK BOUCHER, Virginia
EDOLPHUS TOWNS, New York
FRANK PALLONE, Jr., New Jersey
SHERROD BROWN, Ohio
BART GORDON, Tennessee
BOBBY L. RUSH, Illinois
ANNA G. ESHOO, California
BART STUPAK, Michigan
ELIOT L. ENGEL, New York
ALBERT R. WYNN, Maryland
GENE GREEN, Texas
TED STRICKLAND, Ohio
DIANA DEGETTE, Colorado
LOIS CAPPS, California
MIKE DOYLE, Pennsylvania
TOM ALLEN, Maine
JIM DAVIS, Florida
JAN SCHAKOWSKY, Illinois
HILDA L. SOLIS, California
CHARLES A. GONZALEZ, Texas
JAY INSLEE, Washington
TAMMY BALDWIN, Wisconsin
MIKE ROSS, Arkansas

BUD ALBRIGHT, *Staff Director*
DAVID CAVICKE, *Deputy Staff Director and General Counsel*
REID P.F. STUNTZ, *Minority Staff Director and Chief Counsel*

SUBCOMMITTEE ON HEALTH

NATHAN DEAL, Georgia, *Chairman*

RALPH M. HALL, Texas
MICHAEL BILIRAKIS, Florida
FRED UPTON, Michigan
PAUL E. GILLMOR, Ohio
CHARLIE NORWOOD, Georgia
BARBARA CUBIN, Wyoming
JOHN SHIMKUS, Illinois
JOHN B. SHADEGG, Arizona
CHARLES W. "CHIP" PICKERING, Mississippi
STEVE BUYER, Indiana
JOSEPH R. PITTS, Pennsylvania
MARY BONO, California
MIKE FERGUSON, New Jersey
MIKE ROGERS, Michigan
SUE MYRICK, North Carolina
MICHAEL C. BURGESS, Texas
JOE BARTON, Texas,
(Ex Officio)

SHERROD BROWN, Ohio
Ranking Member
HENRY A. WAXMAN, California
EDOLPHUS TOWNS, New York
FRANK PALLONE, Jr., New Jersey
BART GORDON, Tennessee
BOBBY L. RUSH, Illinois
ANNA G. ESHOO, California
GENE GREEN, Texas
TED STRICKLAND, Ohio
DIANA DEGETTE, Colorado
LOIS CAPPS, California
TOM ALLEN, Maine
JIM DAVIS, Florida
TAMMY BALDWIN, Wisconsin
JOHN D. DINGELL, Michigan,
(Ex Officio)

Steve doesn't take drugs, so why should he have to pay for someone else's drug abuse treatment? Okay. Steve does, however, struggle with depression, but Ann doesn't. So why should she have to pay for Steve's medication and therapy? Ann does, however, have diabetes, but Joe doesn't. So why should Joe have to pay for Ann's diabetes supplies? Joe however, does have terminal cancer, but Steve doesn't. So why should he have to help pay for Joe's cancer medication?

In nearly all cases benefit mandates compensate for one of three problems in the health care market:

One, the slippery slope. That is when society decides that some health care needs are legitimate and others aren't.

Two, you could be next. That is when healthy people forget that their luck could in fact change.

Three, not in my backyard. That is when you truly believe there should be coverage for high-risk individuals as long as they aren't in your plan.

Maybe you believe in high-risk pools, but not in government programs. Individual tax credits, MSAs, association health plans, now the Health Care Choice Act: These aren't insurance proposals. Insurance isn't a gated community for the healthy; it is a safe harbor for the sick. Like MSAs, HPs and the like, this proposal seems to be based on the decisive and dangerous premise that some people matter and some people don't. When it comes to hurricanes, the sick should matter the most.

Thank you, Mr. Chairman.

Mr. DEAL. Thank you, Mr. Brown.

I will now call on Mr. Shadegg, the author of the legislation, for his opening statement.

Mr. SHADEGG. Thank you, Mr. Chairman. Let me begin by thanking you for holding this hearing on this innovative piece of legislation. I also would like to thank all of our witnesses.

I particularly want to note former Congressman Mike Kreidler. It is always nice to have a former colleague come back. There is life after Congress.

Today, as you noted, there are 45 millions without health insurance. Two-thirds of those uninsured have incomes below 200 percent of the Federal poverty level. Most cite unaffordability as the top reason for why they are uninsured. We can do something about this problem. The Health Care Choice Act will both help reduce bureaucracy and harness market forces to lower the cost of hurricanes and, most importantly, reduce the number of uninsured.

As Speaker Hastert said, we shouldn't be forcing people to buy a Cadillac when all they need is a Chevy. At this point, let me talk briefly about the opening comments of my colleague, Mr. Brown.

Yes, mandates in some instances may be appropriate. Mr. Hastert's comment about forcing people to buy a Cadillac, not a Chevy, may be inaccurate in some regards. But New York, for example, requires the coverage of podiatrists. Eleven States require the coverage of acupuncturists. Four States require the coverage of massage therapists.

There are, clearly, mandated benefits that are not necessary and are driving up the cost of health insurance. In 1965, in America, there were only seven benefit mandates in all of the States. Today there are more than 1,800.

In some markets this has helped create a situation where rates in one State can be as much as 75 percent higher than rates in the neighboring State, and people are shopping with their feet. They are literally going to a neighboring State, finding a friend or a relative, and registering as though—or applying for insurance as though they lived in that neighboring State. That simply doesn't make any sense and we need to fix it.

For example, in New Jersey, the average cost for a single person to buy health insurance is over $4,000 a year. Right across the river in Pennsylvania, the average cost is less than $1,500 a year.

This bill will give consumers the option of buying health insurance that meets their needs and is right for them. It also lowers health insurance costs by cutting red tape. The result, it will result in significant cost savings. A recent study found that consumers would save an estimated 77 percent in New Jersey, 22 percent in Washington, 21 percent in Oregon and 16 percent in Maryland if those States eliminated just some of their mandates.

It is important to note the Health Care Choice Act does not eliminate consumer protection or decrease it. I would like to make a point of what it does do.

For example, insurers must be licensed in the primary State. They must get the insurance product approved by that State. They must meet all of that State's laws and requirements before they can sell in a secondary State. They must meet a risk-based capital standard for determining solvency. That is the NAIC's gold standard for determining solvency.

They must provide all policyholders with access to external review, an issue that my colleague, Congressman Norwood, and I worked on in the Patient's Bill of Rights. They must incorporate significant disclosure, and this is the form they must provide not only when they sell the policy, but in each and every renewal notice. I think we are all very familiar with the renewal notices we get on a very regular basis; the disclosure must be in that document.

They must provide each secondary State with a copy of the policy. They must provide written notice of their compliance—to the secondary State of their compliance with of the laws of the primary State, and they must provide financial information on a quarterly basis to each secondary State.

The secondary States may assess premiums and other taxes, including high-risk pool assessments, a companion piece of legislation, which I look forward to moving with this bill. They must conduct—they may conduct a financial review of the insurer if the primary State did not do so.

They may require compliance with any lawful order which they issue. They may seek an injunction alleging that the insurer is in hazardous financial condition. They may require participation in the secondary States guaranty fund. They may require compliance with the secondary State's fraud and abuse laws.

They may require compliance with the secondary State's unfair claims settlement practice laws. They may require that all insurance brokers and agents be licensed in their State, and they may stop the sale of insurance to groups or individuals not permitted or by an insurer in hazardous financial condition.

I believe this bill strikes an appropriate balance, maintaining State regulation without moving that regulation to Washington DC, like other reform proposals that are on the table, while at the same time increasing consumer access to affordable health insurance.

Finally, I would like to note that with the addition of Ed Towns of our committee, this legislation is bipartisan in its sponsorship. I hope it will ultimately be even more so. I believe this is an innovative idea that deserves examination.

I look forward to the testimony of our witnesses, and again, Mr. Chairman, I would like to thank that you for holding the hearing.

Mr. DEAL. I thank the gentleman.

I recognize the ranking member of the committee, Mr. Dingell, for his opening statement.

Mr. DINGELL. Mr. Chairman, thank you for your courtesy.

Before I begin my statement, I would like to welcome an old friend of many members of this committee, a former colleague of ours on this committee and in the Congress, a distinguished, able and dedicated member of this body when he served here, the Honorable Mike Kreidler, who is going to be testifying before us today.

Mike, welcome back.

You follow, interestingly enough, in a distinguished office and another old friend of mine whose name you probably don't know, but Joel Lewnham, who is an insurance commissioner in your State also. So welcome back.

And thank you for that, Mr. Chairman.

Now, with regard to the specific legislation today, we are going to find today that there will be raised broad issues about health care costs as they rise, affordability of health care insurance, the coverage of Americans seeking individual policies and consumer protections that accompany that insurance coverage. Some of the witnesses who appear before the subcommittee today will believe that if insurance companies could limit the number of protections provided by States to their residents, the price of coverage would drop and more people would be insured.

This argument ignores the broader picture. State regulation is vital to protect those who reside in that State from unscrupulous actors and to protect those who would otherwise have no protection.

I want to make it clear that my opposition to this legislation in no way affects the high respect or the great affection I have for the author of the legislation. But this committee has studied these kinds of matters in earlier days; we went into the problems that exist with regard to State insurance regulation.

The purpose of State insurance regulation is to assure, first of all, that the insurance companies are solvent; second of all, to assure that persons who are insured have the ability to have their claims adjudicated honorably and fairly. It is not really about price controls, and we have found that the insurance industry is very much plagued by irresponsible, evil, unprincipled, and scoundrelly individuals who traffic across State lines to the great disadvantage of everyone.

We found that the State regulatory agencies are incapable of addressing these matters and that people would leave this country with suitcases full of money that they had stolen from ratepayers and from insurance policy owners, and that they had defaulted on the payment of bills in the most scandalous way. We found that there is great need, rather than to weaken State regulation to, in fact, strengthen State regulation for the protection of persons who are dependent upon these kinds of insurance for something which is of vital importance to them.

Reduced insurance premiums for some people are little consolation for the consumers who, under this bill, would be left without coverage or left in the hands of State regulatory agencies, which would be incapable of affording those covered with the insurance which they desperately need.

Reduced insurance premiums would mean little to the person who no longer has coverage for critically needed benefit such as diabetes care or maternity care or breast cancer treatment. Insurance companies would be empowered to avoid caring for the sick people who cut into their profit margin and, thus, to essentially select by a process of cherry-picking or cream-skimming those who afford them the greatest opportunity for profit and the least opportunity for payoff and payout.

This legislation would also greatly increase opportunity for mischief. To expect one State insurance commissioner to regulate the operations of an insurance company in 50 States, which may or may not even be located in the United States, but might be located offshore in one of the Caribbean islands is, I think, rather too much hope and trust for the situation that we have found to be the case in the insurance industry. Indeed, it would be a little bit like using one pat of butter for a whole loaf of bread.

It would spread the coverage, the protection and the insurance too thinly to assure any good for anyone; and without adequate oversight, trouble is almost certain to arrive. As a matter of fact, all you have to do is look to see what is happening now in the industry to understand the parallel that exists with regard to persons if this were to occur. You will find that the State insurance commissioners are desperately fearful of this kind of legislation worsening the situation. There are already almost insurmountable tasks and burdens.

I want to agree with my good friend and sponsor in his desire to make health coverage more affordable for the uninsured. I have introduced a number of bills on this matter, as have most of us in this Congress. But I am concerned that the solution proposed in the Health Care Choice Act may worsen the situation and not better it from the standpoint of consumers or from the standpoint of intelligent regulation which protects our people from serious wrongdoing and from rascals who have been able to exploit the weakness of the current system to their great economic success.

We do need to address the issue of affordability of health insurance, but the solution lies in looking at health care costs, not taking away heartfelt consumer State protections from those who are sickest, weakest or who have the least means to address the problem.

We also need to look more closely at the availability of health insurance coverage. With the number of uninsured on the rise, this problem is going to grow, as it is now. But insurance that does not cover the benefits you need is no better than having no insurance at all.

I would hope that collectively we could find a better way to take care of our citizens than leaving them at the mercy of insurance companies' bottom lines, now inadequately covered by State regulation and covered under this legislation under still weaker and more unfortunate kinds of protections for the consumers.

Thank you, Mr. Chairman.

Mr. DEAL. I thank the gentleman.

I recognize my colleague from Georgia, Dr. Norwood.

Mr. NORWOOD. Thank you very much, Mr. Chairman. I ask your indulgence this morning. I am testing a new medical device that would be very helpful to people who might need a little extra oxygen, but I am not sure what it will do to the microphones yet.

I thank you for calling this hearing on the Health Care Choice Act. I wanted to start by stating my support for this legislation as a good discussion starter. We all believe in giving working-class Americans every opportunity to obtain the health care coverage that is sometimes just out of reach. But we need to become creative. It is refreshing and encouraging to see us thinking outside the box, and I commend my friend, Mr. Shadegg.

As we all well know, the increasing cost of health care has affected millions of Americans. Across the board, the premium for health care insurance has skyrocketed. Congress now must act in a way that will increase the affordability and accessibility of health care to all of our citizens.

The number of people without health insurance has been rising now for decades. Many do not have coverage through their jobs. Some of those that do can't afford their premiums. The number of uninsured Americans is obviously too high and underscores the need for a change in the way we think about delivering health insurance. And we can't forget the small businesses that simply cannot afford coverage at today's prices.

Uninsured Americans face serious hurdles in entering the insurance marketplace. For most, the high cost of health insurance is all it takes to limit access. That is where tools like tax incentives and health savings accounts can be of real help, but we need to deal further. Right now, individuals can only purchase health insurance from companies whose policies are approved for sale in their State. This legislation would change that and would offer consumers much more choice.

This bill will allow individuals to buy insurance from insurance companies based in other States who choose to market regionally or nationally. Such a change could spark some innovation in the insurance marketplace. If people could get health insurance cheaper across State lines, fewer people would go without it; consumers, not politicians, would help determine what policy benefits they wish to get in order to help get market forces moving.

This legislation contains many protections to guarantee that an insurer has to follow all the laws of the State they are primarily established in, and that is a good start. They would also be responsible to the State insurance commissioner and would have to meet every requirement under every State law or under that State's law. Furthermore, the insurer is subject to regulation in each and every secondary State.

However, we need to make sure that we don't end up limiting sicker patients and those with preexisting conditions to a few high-risk pools or insurers that specialize in such cases. First steps are made in that regard by outlawing re-underwriting.

Most importantly, all policies will include some safeguards not present in all States. This bill requires each policyholder to be able to appeal medical decisions to a panel of independent health professionals. It still baffles me that eight States do not allow independent review for policyholders. This bill does a lot of good in this area.

But I would like to make this bill even better by getting a few more patient protections in it, including some more language dealing with external review provisions. That said, this bill is a great start, and I look forward to working with my friend, Mr. Shadegg.

Mr. Chairman, I yield back.

Mr. DEAL. I thank the gentleman.

I now recognize the gentleman from New Jersey, Mr. Pallone.

Mr. PALLONE. Thank you, Mr. Chairman.

I want to voice my strong opposition to the Health Care Choice Act. It is a terrible bill in my opinion from a public health perspective, and would do nothing to lower the cost of health insurance or reduce the number of uninsured Americans. In fact, if enacted, the H.R. 2355 would only serve to worsen these problems.

The bill seeks to allow insurance companies to select a State in which they want to be regulated and then sell their product in other States. Proponents of the bill would have us believe that this would result in a greater variety of insurance products for consumers to choose from at a lower cost. But in reality this bill will result in a race to the bottom as insurers try to set up shops in States with fewer consumer protections.

Such a proposal would have a particularly disastrous effect in my home State of New Jersey, essentially rendering our consumer protections meaningless and destroying our individual insurance market.

Every State in the U.S. has enacted insurance reforms that have been developed to provide stability and certain protections for consumers in the insurance market. Some States offer more protection than others.

In my home State of New Jersey, we have enacted extensive reforms that go beyond what many other States offer, including guaranteed issue and renewal, community rating and standardization of benefit plans. Thanks to these consumer protections, New Jersey is able to ensure that its residents have access to quality individual insurance products. H.R. 2355 will completely undermine that promise, in my opinion.

In New Jersey, insurers cannot turn people away because of risk factors such as health status, age, gender, occupation or geographic location. Every New Jersey resident can access coverage at a similar price regardless of risk.

In order for New Jersey to guarantee access to this kind of insurance, it must be able to spread risk throughout the market. That means pooling low and high risks together. If H.R. 2355 were enacted, it would completely dismantle New Jersey's existing risk pool. Younger and healthier consumers would flee New Jersey's market in order to obtain cheaper policies that provide less coverage, leaving only high-risk consumers in the market.

In addition, high risks residing in other States without generous consumer protections, like Arizona, for example, Mr. Shadegg's State, would probably select insurance plans regulated by New Jersey if there were any to remain at all. Without any low-risk left to cross-subsidize the high-risk, premiums would likely rise and become unaffordable. New Jersey could not sustain an individual market under these conditions and would likely be thrown into a death spiral, leaving our most sick and vulnerable citizens with few places to turn to get health coverage.

Now, someone here today—and I think Mr. Shadegg was sort of alluding to that—will try to convince this committee that because of such consumer protections, individual insurance in New Jersey is expensive and unaffordable for many of its residents. Now it is true that the cost of insurance is slightly more expensive in New Jersey, but that is because it is a better product.

Furthermore, according to the Kaiser Family Foundation, 14 percent of New Jersey's population currently does not have health insurance. Now you compare that to Arizona, which has fewer consumer protections and presumably less costly insurance, but 17 percent of the population currently has no insurance in Arizona. So this leads me to believe that consumer protections are not the culprit behind the rising costs of health insurance, and circumventing them will not lower the price of insurance.

I think, Mr. Chairman, that the bill we are considering today is simply a ruse. The bill would be more appropriately entitled the Health Care Choice Unless You Are Old and Sick Act. This bill does nothing to lower the cost of health insurance or extend coverage to the people who need it most. If enacted, it would only result in more people purchasing low-cost health plans that offer limited coverage and carry big risks. While these people would be technically considered insured, it would be meaningless because their policies would not cover much if they ever got sick.

If we are serious about lowering the cost of health insurance and extending coverage to the 45 million or more uninsured Americans, then we should address what is the driving cost of health care instead of enacting meaningless reform that would worsen matters. We should push for new laws that better control overall health care costs and expand access to quality health insurance for more Americans, especially our most vulnerable populations.

I yield back.

Mr. DEAL. I recognize the gentleman from Indiana, Mr. Buyer.

Mr. BUYER. I would just like to hear from the witnesses. I yield back.

Mr. DEAL. I recognize Ms. Baldwin.

Ms. BALDWIN. Thank you, Mr. Chairman.

While applauding the author's intentions in offering this legislation, I have serious concerns about the bill that we are discussing today. I strongly believe that all Americans have a right to affordable, quality and comprehensive health care.

As many on this panel have already emphasized, 45 million Americans are uninsured, and many millions more are underinsured. Earlier this month, the Commonwealth Fund released a study estimating that there are 16 million Americans who are underinsured, meaning their insurance did not adequately protect them against catastrophic health care expenses.

That means 61 million Americans either have no insurance, sporadic insurance or have coverage that leaves them exposed to high health care costs. Sixty-one million Americans is nearly 21 percent of our population, one in five. Clearly this is unacceptable, and I would very much like to have this committee search out ways to address this crisis.

I do not believe that H.R. 2355 would do the job. While purporting to make health care more affordable, I believe it would create, as my colleague just said, a race to the bottom, where insurers will offer stripped-down health insurance products by evading consumer protections that have been put in place by the States. Consumers who choose these cheap products will be left without important protections while those who do not choose these products will see their own health care premiums rise due to adverse selection. We will end up with more uninsured and more underinsured Americans.

Mr. Chairman, the underlying issues that we are talking about today—uninsurance, underinsurance, affordability and quality—are critical, and I hope our subcommittee will have, in the future, the chance to discuss other approaches to address these very severe problems.

I yield back.

Mr. DEAL. Thank the gentlelady.

I recognize Mr. Green from Texas for an opening statement.

Mr. GREEN. Thank you, Mr. Chairman.

Like my colleagues, I would like to welcome Mike Kreidler back. You know, it is interesting; we were elected, I guess, in 1992, Congresswoman Eshoo; and again going from a Member of Congress to a Commissioner of Insurance in Washington, that may be a step up. I am wondering. Having served in the legislature in Texas for many years and dealing with our insurance commissioners at that time, it is almost as tough a job as any.

But, Mr. Chairman, I want to thank you for calling the hearing on the Health Care Choice Act. Again, I, like my colleagues, want to thank our colleague, Mr. Shadegg, for introducing the legislation.

We have long showed how best to provide affordable health insurance to all Americans to decrease the numbers uninsured in our country. My State of Texas has the unfortunate distinction of having the highest number of uninsured individuals in the Nation. There is always an increase in our utilization for nonemergency conditions while increasing health care costs for all individuals.

In a recent study, Families USA concluded that the cost of treating the uninsured has led to an annual premium of $1,550 for the average Texas family. Without question, Congress must act to provide affordable health insurance to the ununinsured and underinsured in our country.

I question whether our enactment of this bill is the right action to take. By allowing an uninsured to set up shop in one State to provide health insurance to a beneficiary in another, this bill introduces a host of problems and risks for the consumer. There is a point at which inadequate health insurance may be just as bad as no health insurance at all for a consumer. This bill may open the door for that dangerous scenario to become a reality.

I fear the Health Care Choice Act offers more choice to the health insurer than to the beneficiary. The bill gives health insurers the opportunity to shop around and settle in what State has the fewest consumer protections.

It is really a simple business decision. Every business seeks to operate in the most favorable business climate, and this legislation would allow health insurers to do that. The problem is consumers lose out on the protections that been they may have been granted undertheir own State law.

In Texas, if a Texan buys a policy regulated in Alabama, he is protected by Alabama laws and not Texas laws. If the Texas consumer protection laws are stronger, then that policyholder is out of luck. To make matters worse, he cannot use his voting power to help change those laws that protect him because his vote has no effect in Alabama.

In my State of Texas we have some of the highest rates of diabetes in the country. We also have State diabetes requirements that mandate health insurance coverage of diabetes testing supplies, insulin, syringes and diabetes education.

Under this bill, health insurers could easily leave the State of Texas, set up a shop in any one of four States without State diabetes requirements, leaving many Texans without the coverage for supplies and medication to help them manage this life-threatening disease.

While this bill's overall goal is to reduce the number of uninsured, an unfortunate unintended consequence could be to increase the number of underinsured.

I look forward to hearing from our witnesses. Hopefully, we can work it out. But I want to look at any avenue we can for increasing our opportunities to cover people with our insurance system, but also not make it to where they don't receive anything but a quality product for what they pay.

Thank you, Mr. Chairman.

Mr. DEAL. I thank the gentleman. I recognize the chairman of the full committee, Mr. Barton from Texas, for an opening statement.

Chairman BARTON. Thank you, Chairman Deal, for holding this hearing today. Last year, 45 million Americans lacked health insurance for at least some part of the year. Millions went without health insurance because there was no policy that they could afford. This is not a new problem.

Each year, when the Census Bureau announces its health insurance statistics, activists stampede to demand that the government take over and run the health care system. See, they say, the market doesn't work. Their view is, if only everybody could have something like Medicaid, America would be happier and healthier.

They are wrong, America's health system doesn't have a market problem; it has a government problem. Both the system and the uninsured are afflicted by the consequences of years and years of government meddling at both the State and Federal level—too many regulations, too many subsidies, too many mandates and too many policies that are supposed to improve health insurance. These efforts have combined to distort the market and make it very difficult for average working-class Americans to purchase reasonably priced health insurance.

Look at what happens when you compare the average monthly premiums in different States. In my home State of Texas, for example, the average premium for a single policy is $133 a month. In New Jersey, that same policy costs $340 a month. The difference is $2,400 a year.

Some people might be able to reach in their pockets and just pluck out an extra $2,400, but not many working people can do that. They are the ones who most often resolve the problem by deciding that groceries and rent are more important than an insurance policy. So they buy their groceries and pay their rent and pray that they won't get sick or hurt. H.R. 2355, the Health Care Choice Act, addresses these problems by allowing people to buy health insurance across the State lines.

I want to thank my good friend, John Shadegg, for introducing this piece of legislation. My understanding is that Congressman Ed Towns has also endorsed it and has become a sponsor of it.

Allowing people to purchase a health insurance policy they can really afford goes a long way toward reducing the number of uninsured. It is a little less government, a little more freedom. That makes a big difference.

I look forward to hearing from today's witnesses on this proposal. It is my hope that this hearing will allow us to examine the legislation and assess its impact on consumers, States and insurance markets and ultimately the cost of health insurance. If the hearing goes as well as I hope it goes, there is a good chance we could be marking this piece of legislation up in the very near future.

Thank you, Chairman Deal, for holding today's hearing. I yield back the balance of my time.

Mr. DEAL. I thank the gentleman.

I recognize the gentlelady from California, Ms. Eshoo, for an opening statement.

Ms. ESHOO. Good morning, Mr. Chairman. Thank you for holding this hearing.

And welcome to our, witnesses and most especially, our former colleague and good friend and classmate, Mike Kreidler. I am looking forward to hearing your testimony this morning.

I think that we are all absolutely in favor of making insurance, health insurance, more affordable for people in our country. I think that that is the intent of the gentleman's legislation. But I do think that it has flaws in it. Whether it—I would say unintentionally—brings about some effect, I don't really think the American people are going to weigh in and say, This is really going to be terrific for us.

The effects of the legislation, I think, would be rather harmful in many areas. First of all, it allows insurers to choose States that have the most lenient rules, which then would eliminate some of the most, I think, key consumer protections that States have seen fit to make part of what is offered to people and to protect them.

It could eliminate coverage of screening of mammography and cervical cancer, coverage for cancer, clinical trials, direct access to OB/GYNs, mental health parity; and in my home State of California, the ability of California regulators to help resolve complaints by consumers who purchase coverage from an insurer licensed in another State. That could just be wiped out.

So while I think that the gentleman's intention of enabling people to have health care insurance coverage and at a good rate, the language is really structured in a way that I think most people really would not weigh in and say, I want that.

I really look forward to Commissioner Kreidler's testimony today on how he would protect consumers in his State of Washington from fraud and unpaid or disputed claims if the insurer is licensed by the laws of a second State and domiciled in a third State.

You know, on the surface of these things, obviously, the advertising, so to speak, is really engaging, as well as it should be. But I think that we have to understand very clearly how this would work.

I would also add—and this will be the last part of my statement—that States, I think, have filled in many situations the void that exists with a real national policy on health care, on insurance and on coverage for all people.

In saying that, of course, it is more expensive to do business in New Jersey than it is in some mostly rural States because urban areas are simply more expensive to do business in. It is not just the cost of the insurance policy. Everything is more expensive.

I can tell you that it is far more expensive in the San Francisco Bay Area than it is in the Central Valley, which is mostly agricultural, in the State of California. So there are differences in these markets that we need to take into consideration.

Last, our distinguished chairman of the full committee said, a little less government and more freedom. I think that people—that the American people are all for freedom. But I also think that they want to be—have the protection, the consumer protections that have been hard fought and won in so many different places in the country; and most importantly, that those consumer protections have really made a key and profound effect in people's lives.

So, thank you, Mr. Chairman, for having this hearing. I think that we have a very interesting debate here. I think that our witnesses are well chosen and are going to bring much to it. Thank you.

Mr. DEAL. I thank the gentlelady.

I recognize Dr. Burgess for an opening statement.

Mr. BURGESS. Mr. Chairman, I will submit my statement for the record in the interest of time.

Mr. DEAL. I thank the gentleman.

The chairman recognizes Ms. Myrick for an opening statement.

Mrs. MYRICK. I will waive. Thank you.

Mr. DEAL. Thank you, I believe that concludes our opening statements, I am pleased to introduce our distinguished panel members to the audience and to the members of the committee.

First of all, Dr. Merrill Matthews, Jr., who is the Director of the Council for Affordable Health Insurance; Mr. Robert de Posada, who is Chairman and President of The Latino Coalition; of course, he has already been introduced several times, our former colleague, Mr. Mike Kreidler, who is now the Insurance Commissioner for the State of Washington and representing the National Association of Insurance Commissioners; Mr. Limbaugh, Mr. Hunter Limbaugh, who is the Chief of the Advocacy Committee of the American Diabetes Association; and Dr. David Gratzer, who is a Senior Fellow from the Manhattan Institute.

Gentlemen, we are pleased to have you today. Your written testimony has been a made a part of the record.

We will ask you for 5 minutes, if you would, to summarize the essence of your testimony. We will follow that with questions from the committee.

Dr. Matthews, you are first.

STATEMENTS OF MERRILL MATTHEWS, JR., DIRECTOR, COUNCIL FOR AFFORDABLE HEALTH INSURANCE; ROBERT GARCIA de POSADA, CHAIRMAN/PRESIDENT, THE LATINO COALITION; MIKE KREIDLER, WASHINGTON STATE INSURANCE COMMISSIONER, ON BEHALF OF THE NATIONAL ASSOCIATION OF INSURANCE COMMISSIONERS; L. HUNTER LIMBAUGH, CHAIR, ADVOCACY COMMITTEE, AMERICAN DIABETES ASSOCIATION; AND DAVID GRATZER, SENIOR FELLOW, THE MANHATTAN INSTITUTE

Mr. MATTHEWS. Good morning, Mr. Chairman and members of the subcommittee. I am pleased to be here.

I want to thank the chairman of the subcommittee for calling this very important hearing today on the Health Care Choice Act. I commend your leadership for considering ways, innovative ways, that would allow millions of Americans, uninsured Americans, to have access to affordable health insurance.

I am Merrill Matthews, Director of the Council for Affordable Health Insurance, which is a research and advocacy association of insurance carriers, active, individual, small group market, health savings accounts, senior markets and others. In summarizing my points, I would like to make three primary points.

The growing cost of health insurance and its effect on the uninsured: Health care costs are growing. In a recent study from Health Affairs, health care spending is up by 8.2 percent in 2004, growing faster than the rate of inflation. When health care cost spending goes up, health insurance premiums go up, and that has a direct effect on the number of uninsured, leading to our 45 million Americans without health insurance.

Frankly, the States have not been all that helpful in trying to address this problem. One thing they have done, already mentioned, is the health insurance mandates. Forty years ago, there was just a handful of mandates around the country. Today, according to our count at the Council, we find 1,824 mandates around the country.

We have, Mr. Chairman, over there I believe, a copy of our publication, which tracks each of the mandates in each of the States. We also went through and had a group of actuaries assess what they thought the basic cost of those mandates was and would be in general. Our estimate is that the mandates in the States increase the cost of health insurance roughly 20 to 50 percent, depending upon the State that you live in.

In addition, there are the guaranteed issue and community rating laws that eight different States have passed. That has made health insurance unaffordable in several States. New Jersey was mentioned earlier.

If you go on the State's Web site, a Plan D policy, that is, a $500 deductible, 20 percent copayment, is going to cost, for a family, roughly $3,912 a month from Oxford Health Insurance. That is the least expensive policy. That is a monthly premium. It is on the State's Web site. If you want to look at Aetna's Plan D policy, family policy, $500 deductible, 20 percent copayment, you are looking at $6,025 a month.

You do have guarantees in New Jersey, but you don't have a guarantee that people can afford it, and they can't. High-risk pools, we believe, are a much better way of addressing that.

Health insurance premiums vary by State. eHealthInsurance, which is an online marketer of health insurance, tracks the policies that are being sold through that Web site. When you look at that—and we have a chart over here; it is also reproduced in my testimony before you—New Jersey is the highest State, $4,080 a year. That is for a single individual, and that is their experience of what people are paying. That is different from what the State puts on the Web site.

Contrast that with what you see in Iowa, $1,236 a year for an individual; Wyoming, $1,284. Is it a difference of where a person lives? The average in the country is $1,800, but even California is only $1,680. Expensive California is less than half what it is in New Jersey.

Go across the State line in Pennsylvania, and you will find a health insurance policy for a third, maybe a fourth of what you would be paying for it in New Jersey.

The health insurance marketplace is changing. What we are talking about is already beginning to happen in many ways. For example, I work at the Council. I actually live in Texas. I live in Dallas, so I am one of your neighbors there. I don't have the health insurance policy provided through the Council, which is based in Virginia. If I did, I would have a Virginia policy with Virginia mandates overseeing me in Texas. That already happens.

In addition, individuals who are looking for individual policies out there are increasingly joining associations. Some of those associations are national; some of them are local like a State local Chamber of Commerce, that sell health insurance. Many States, even though they regulate those association policies, don't regulate them to the same extent that they do individual policies. As a result, millions of Americans are able to buy health insurance out there from a health insurance company that is domiciled in a different State that has some State regulation over that policy, but they are able to get less expensive policies because those health association policies don't always have the mandates included in them.

The point is that despite concerns that the Health Care Choice Act could disrupt the current system and deprive States of their ability to oversee health insurance and protect consumers and generally undermine it, the market is already moving in the direction of trying to find more innovative ways for people to buy health insurance.

What is going to be the impact of the Health Care Choice Act? Well, nearly 90 percent of the people who have private health insurance, that is, working Americans, get it through their employer. I expect this would have very little impact or no impact at all on them.

There are also millions of Americans who currently buy health insurance in their State and are satisfied with it. My wife and youngest daughter, we live in Texas, we have a high deductible Blue Cross policy in Texas. We are satisfied with that policy. It is a fairly affordable policy. If the Health Care Choice Act were to pass, I doubt we would change what we are doing.

That addresses the issue of whether or not this is going to be a race to the bottom. Consumers aren't like that.

When we bought that health insurance policy, we had a range of different policies we could have bought there in Texas. We chose a Blue Cross policy. If the Health Care Choice Act becomes law, we might be able to find a less expensive policy in another State. I don't expect we will do that. We are satisfied with what we have.

The key point is that uninsured Americans out there, especially those living in the high-cost States, would have access to affordable policies that they don't have access to now. Those are people outside the system. They are not being protected by any consumer laws because they aren't in the system, and this gives them a chance to move into it.

We are not advocating the dissolution of the State regulatory system over health insurance. We are advocating an option and health care choices for millions of individual Americans who are currently uninsured because they cannot afford all the services and the protections prescribed by the State.

Thank you, Mr. Chairman.

[The prepared statement of Merrill Matthews follows:]

Statement of Merrill Matthews, Ph.D.
Director, Council for Affordable Health Insurance

Testimony Before the Subcommittee on Health Committee on Energy and Commerce U.S. House of Representatives Tuesday, June 28, 2005

Good morning Mr. Chairman and members of the subcommittee. I am pleased to be here, and I want to thank the Chairman and the subcommittee for calling this very important hearing today on the Health Care Choice Act. I commend your leadership for considering ways that would allow millions of uninsured Americans to have access to affordable health insurance.

I am Merrill Matthews, Ph.D., director of the Council for Affordable Health Insurance (CAHI), which is located in Alexandria, Virginia. CAHI is a research and advocacy association of insurance carriers active in the individual, small group, Health Savings Account and senior markets. CAHI's membership includes health insurance companies, small businesses, physicians, actuaries and insurance brokers. Since 1992, CAHI has been an advocate for market-oriented solutions to the problems in America's health care system.

We at the Council for Affordable Health Insurance believe that all Americans should have access to affordable health coverage. The Health Care Choice Act would go a long way toward reaching that goal.

The Act allows individuals to purchase health insurance coverage across state lines. It requires that the state law where the policy is filed (primary state) would apply both in that state as well as any other state (secondary state). Other consumer protections include requirements regarding disclosure, fraud and abuse, prohibition against "bait and switch" tactics, financial stability of the insurance company and ensuring an independent review mechanism for all who purchase coverage under the terms of this legislation.

In my testimony today, I would like to address three issues regarding (1) the cost of health insurance and the uninsured; (2) state actions that have frequently exacerbated the problem, making health insurance even more expensive; and, (3) the way the health insurance industry is evolving to provide consumers with affordable options.

I. The Growing Cost of Health Insurance and Its Effect on the Uninsured.

Everyone knows that health care costs have been rising.

- According to a new study in the journal *Health Affairs*, health care spending rose 8.2 percent in 2004, down slightly from 8.4 percent in 2003 and 10.7 percent in 2002. So while we are trending in the right direction, several years of health care spending increases three-plus times the rate of inflation has made health insurance very expensive for American families. [1]

- There is some good news: the rapid rise of consumer driven plans appears to be slowing the trend or reducing the cost of health insurance. The *Wall Street Journal* reported on June 14 that data from 13,500 participants in Aetna consumer driven plans showed that companies that offered a consumer driven plan as an option saw their premium increases slow to 3.7 percent, while those companies that offered only a consumer driven plan saw their costs fall by 11 percent.[2]

The rising cost of health care leads inevitably to the rising cost of health insurance premiums. And the cost of health insurance is one of the primary reasons why we have roughly 45 million uninsured Americans. Unless Americans have access to affordable

---

[1] Bradley C. Strunk, Paul B. Ginsburg and John P. Cookson, "Tracking Health Care Costs: Declining Growth Trend Pauses in 2004," *Health Affairs*, Web Exclusive, June 21, 2005. (http://content.healthaffairs.org/cgi/content/abstract/hlthaff.w5.286)

[2] Venessa Fuhrmans, "Patients Give New Insurance Mixed Reviews," *Wall Street Journal*, June 14, 2005.

coverage, the number of uninsured will only grow — to 56 million by 2013, according to a recent estimate published in *Health Affairs*.[3]

There are several reasons for that rise, including wider access to technology and new health care options. But the states and the federal government also bear a portion of the responsibility.

II. The States' Role in Regulating Health Insurance.

Frankly, when it comes to the high cost of health insurance, the states have only exacerbated the problem.

A. *Health insurance mandates* – For 40 years states increasingly have tried to micromanage health insurance, and premiums have ballooned as a result.

A health insurance "mandate" is a requirement that an insurance company or health plan cover (or offer coverage for) health care providers, benefits and patient populations that health coverage might not normally provide. They include:

- Traditional providers such as chiropractors and podiatrists, but also social workers and massage therapists.
- Benefits such as mammograms, well-child care and even drug and alcohol abuse treatment, but also acupuncture, massage therapies and hair prostheses (wigs, usually for those undergoing radiation and chemotherapy for cancer).
- And populations such as adopted and non-custodial children.

While mandates make health insurance more comprehensive, they also make it more expensive because mandates require insurers to pay for care consumers previously funded out of their own pockets. In some markets, mandated benefits increase the cost of health insurance by as much as 45 or 50 percent.

[3] Todd Gilmer and Richard Kronick, "It's the Premiums Stupid: Projections of the Uninsured Through 2013," *Health Affairs*, Web Exclusive, April 5, 2005. (http://content.healthaffairs.org/cgi/content/abstract/hlthaff.w5.143)

Mandating benefits is like saying to someone in the market for a new car, if you can't afford a Cadillac loaded with options, you have to walk.

So why do so many elected representatives persist in passing mandates? They find it difficult to oppose any legislation that promises enhanced care to potentially motivated voters.

In 1965, only seven benefits were mandated by the states; today, the Council for Affordable Health Insurance has identified 1,824 mandated benefits and providers nationwide.[4] (Available at www.cahi.org.)

Mandates enjoy wide bipartisan support, and some states are much worse than others.

- Minnesota has 62 mandates, the most of any state, Virginia 54, and Florida 50.
- Maryland has 58 mandates, while Washington DC has only 16.
- Texas has 51 mandates, but Alabama has only 18.

Some mandates will have a much larger impact on health insurance costs than others. In order to remind legislators that mandates usually aren't free, the Council solicited input from a group of respected actuaries who estimated how much each mandate could affect the cost of a health insurance policy. Their conclusion is that, depending on the state where one lives, Americans could be paying between roughly 20 percent to 50 percent more for their policies because of state-imposed mandates.

B. Guaranteed issue and community rating — Even more costly than a multitude of mandates is guaranteed issue and community rating. Guaranteed issue requires insurers to accept applicants regardless of their health status (although some guaranteed issue provisions may include certain restrictions). People may forgo insurance coverage when they are in good health and purchase

---

[4] Victoria Craig Bunce and J.P. Wieske, Health Insurance Mandates in the States, 2005" Council for Affordable Health Insurance, January 2005.
(http://www.cahi.org/cahi_contents/resources/pdf/MandatePubDec2004.pdf)

it when they are sick. As a result, the pool gets smaller and the insurance more expensive because young and/or healthy people drop out of the pool, knowing they can return when they get sick.

Guaranteed issue is even more destructive when combined with community rating, which requires an insurer to charge the same price to everyone in a "community," or pool, regardless of the differences in the risk the individuals present. Age, lifestyle, health and gender factors may not be used to determine rates. In other words, everyone can get a policy at roughly the same price. "Modified community rating" will allow some variation in premium, such as for geographic location.

Several states passed guaranteed issue and community rating legislation in the early 1990s, destroying those states' individual health insurance markets.

New Jersey is the poster child for how not to reform the health care system. When New Jersey's guaranteed issue legislation became effective in 1994, a family policy (known as "Plan D") with a $500 deductible and a 20 percent copayment (i.e., the insurer pays 80 percent) cost as little as $463 a month and as much as $1,076, depending on which of the 14 participating insurers the family chose, according to the New Jersey Department of Insurance. Today, *the lowest monthly premium* for a family Plan D policy is $3,912, offered by Oxford.

Monthly premiums for family coverage under an Aetna Plan D policy, the least costly after Oxford, rose from $769 in 1994 to $6,025 today, a stunning 683 percent increase. Remember, that's the *monthly* premium.

Supporters of guaranteed issue say it is necessary to make coverage accessible to those who need it most. But state-sponsored high-risk pools are the best way to make coverage accessible to the medically uninsurable. High-risk pools act as a safety net for people who are uninsurable, or whose premiums cost more than the standard. Established more than 25 years ago, high-risk pools operate in 33 states and covered more than 181,000 people as of June 2004, according to Communicating for Agriculture.[5]

In most states with high-risk pools, applicants have a choice among HMOs or PPOs, and most offer a range of deductibles and copays. In other words, applicants can choose what best fits their needs and budget. State high-risk pools are usually funded by assessing health insurers operating within a state, based on the amount of business the insurer writes. Some states have relied on other funding sources such as lotteries or general tax revenues.

However, in 2002 Congress passed legislation that provided federal money (through 2004) to be used for start-up costs in states where no high-risk pool existed. The legislation further provided funds for states that already had operational high-risk pools, so long as currently existing pools were consistent with regulatory guidelines.

Congress should continue to provide federal funding for these state risk pools, since that is the most efficient way to provide a safety net for the uninsurable while letting the private sector work for most other Americans.

The evidence from guaranteed issue states is in; we have all the data we need. Not one experiment has proved successful. Several more states have tried variations of these requirements, such as modified community rating. But these efforts only "modify" the full damage. States need either to eliminate these destructive regulations, or Congress needs to let families buy their coverage from a state that hasn't destroyed its market.

C. The eHealthInsurance survey of premiums. eHealthInsurance is an online marketer for health insurance. The company tracks hundreds of thousands of individuals purchasing coverage and how much they pay in premiums. (See the table below, especially bold figures.) For example, an individual living in New Jersey buying coverage for himself (i.e., not a group policy that comes from an employer), pays, on average, about $4,080 a year. (Note: the New Jersey policies

[5] "Comprehensive Health Insurance for High-Risk Individuals — A State-by-State Analysis," Communicating for Agriculture, Inc., Eighteenth Edition, 2004/2005, November 4, 2004.

cited in the previous section were for a specific type of family policy.) That's the highest health insurance premium in the country, according to the survey, with neighboring New York running a close second at $3,540.

However, the average annual premium in Iowa is $1,236 and Wyoming $1,284, the lowest in the country; and it's only $1,800 for the nation as a whole.

Thus, health insurance is roughly 3.5 times more expensive in New Jersey and New York than in Iowa and Wyoming.

Perhaps the difference is that the cost of living is higher in New Jersey and New York. While that may explain some of the variation, it doesn't explain most of it. New Jersey's neighbor Pennsylvania has an average premium of $1,488. Even high-cost California is only $1,680 per year, according to eHealthInsurance — still less than half that of New Jersey and New York.

The point is that health insurance premiums vary significantly by state, leaving thousands of individuals in high-cost states, such as New Jersey, New York and Maine, struggling to find affordable coverage. If they could buy health insurance coverage that is already available to people in another state, millions could leave the ranks of the uninsured.

Health Insurance Premiums for Single Policies by State

State	Population	% of U.S. Population	Avg. monthly premium per single: all ages	Avg. annual premium per single: all ages	Avg. age	Guaranteed Issue (1)	Community Rating (2)
California	34,705,060	12.4%	$140	$1,680	32		
Texas	21,266,000	7.6%	$133	$1,596	33		
New York	**19,027,190**	**6.8%**	**$295**	**$3,540**	**40**	**Yes**	**Yes**
Florida	16,349,150	5.8%	$148	$1,776	34		
Illinois	12,406,690	4.4%	$140	$1,680	33		
Pennsylvania	12,139,190	4.3%	$138	$1,656	31		
Ohio	11,220,060	4.0%	$132	$1,584	34		
Michigan	9,898,680	3.5%	$112	$1,344	33		
New Jersey	**8,521,890**	**3.0%**	**$340**	**$4,080**	**38**	**Yes**	**Yes**
Georgia	8,332,840	3.0%	$159	$1,908	31		
North Carolina	8,071,000	2.9%	$130	$1,560	32		
Virginia	7,022,090	2.5%	$154	$1,848	34		
Indiana	6,060,210	2.2%	$125	$1,500	34		
Washington	5,953,980	2.1%	$169	$2,028	35		
Tennessee	5,662,530	2.0%	$127	$1,524	33		
Missouri	5,552,640	2.0%	$139	$1,668	32		
Wisconsin	5,402,080	1.9%	$126	$1,512	36		
Maryland	5,377,260	1.9%	$166	$1,992	32		
Arizona	5,349,660	1.9%	$153	$1,836	34		
Minnesota	4,983,580	1.8%	$143	$1,716	33		
Colorado	4,409,790	1.6%	$120	$1,440	33		
Alabama	4,408,280	1.6%	$173	$2,076	28		
Louisiana	4,391,090	1.6%	$135	$1,620	30		
South Carolina	3,997,220	1.4%	$138	$1,656	35		
Kentucky	3,996,680	1.4%	$125	$1,500	33		
Oregon	3,477,490	1.2%	$145	$1,740	31		
Oklahoma	3,404,120	1.2%	$134	$1,608	35		
Connecticut	3,378,790	1.2%	$174	$2,088	35		
Iowa	**2,878,650**	**1.0%**	**$103**	**$1,236**	**35**		
Mississippi	2,781,560	1.0%	$131	$1,572	34		
Arkansas	2,657,680	0.9%	$209	$2,496	37		
Kansas	2,641,180	0.9%	$128	$1,536	30		
Utah	2,283,860	0.8%	$114	$1,368	31		
Nevada	2,125,890	0.8%	$155	$1,860	33		
New Mexico	1,820,030	0.6%	$121	$1,452	32		
Nebraska	1,685,440	0.6%	$129	$1,548	32		
Idaho	1,304,910	0.5%	$162	$1,944	36		
Rhode Island	1,047,970	0.4%	$116	$1,392	33		
Montana	893,600	0.3%	$145	$1,740	31		
Delaware	790,930	0.3%	$131	$1,572	34		

South Dakota	740,970	0.3%	$124	$1,488	32			
Alaska	621,520	0.2%	$157	$1,884	36			
Dist. Columbia	561,370	0.2%	$193	$2,316	32			
Wyoming	**485,510**	**0.2%**	**$107**	**$1,284**	**28**			
Subtotal	270,086,310	96.3%	$150	$1,800	33			
States not included:								
State	Population	% of U.S. Population	Avg. monthly premium per single: all ages	Avg. annual premium per single: all ages	Avg. age	Guaranteed Issue (1)	Community Rating (2)	Other (3)
Massachusetts	3,679,620	1.3%	N/A	N/A	N/A	Yes		
West Virginia	1,760,310	0.6%	N/A	N/A	N/A			Yes
Maine	1,270,120	0.5%	N/A	N/A	N/A	Yes	Yes	
New Hampshire	1,259,120	0.4%	N/A	N/A	N/A	Yes	Yes	
Hawaii	1,198,920	0.4%	N/A	N/A	N/A			Yes
North Dakota(4)	619,280	0.2%	N/A	N/A	N/A			Yes
Vermont	611,540	0.2%	N/A	N/A	N/A	Yes	Yes	
Subtotal	**10,398,910**	**3.7%**						
Total US	**280,485,220**							

(1) Law requires all applicants to be issued a policy regardless of health

(2) Law requires policies to be priced independent of age and/or health

(3) State Department of Insurance and/or state-based carriers limits on non-residential broker sales.

(4) Recently added to www.ehealthinsurance.com, average premium and age data not available to date.

Source: eHealthInsurance.

III. The Expansion of Markets.

The Internet has opened access to a world, literally, of new — and old — products and services.

Of course, the U.S. company Ebay is perhaps the best known source for being able to buy virtually anything at a price the consumer is willing to pay. And while Ebay doesn't sell health insurance over the Internet, eHealthInsurance and a few other websites do.

Some fear the Health Care Choice Act will disrupt the current health insurance model, bypassing most state regulations and perhaps even agents. However, this ignores the fact that consumers are already searching for new and innovative ways to purchase health insurance.

The U.S. workforce is much more mobile and decentralized than it was 30 or 40 years ago. The Internet and other communications tools allow millions of workers to live in a different location than where their employer is based. For example, I live in Dallas, Texas, while the Council is headquartered in Alexandria, Virginia.

I don't get my health insurance through the Council, but if I did, it would be from a health insurance company licensed in Virginia, and adhering to Virginia's regulations and mandates: hence a Texan with a Virginia-based and regulated health insurance policy. Sounds a little like the Health Care Choice Act — and that is in practice today.

In addition, one of the fastest growing sectors of the health insurance market is what is known as "association group insurance," in which individuals who are members of an association (e.g., the Chamber of Commerce) are offered health insurance from a state-regulated and fully licensed insurance company. States impose some oversight on these policies, but most impose far fewer restrictions and regulations on association group insurance than they do on a traditional insurance policy sold to individuals. The reduced regulations and the ability to be more flexible and innovative in their policies allow those insurers to keep their premiums low.

So you have an insurance company that is domiciled in one state selling less-regulated, affordable health insurance through an association in almost every state in the country.

The point is that despite concerns that the Health Care Choice Act could disrupt the current system, deprive states of their ability to oversee insurance and protect consumers, and generally undermine the health insurance market, the market is already moving in that general direction.

IV. Impact of the Health Care Choice Act.

What will happen to the insurance market if the Health Care Choice Act passes?

It will likely have little or no impact on small or large group coverage, and that represents nearly 90 percent of the under-age-65 people who have private (i.e., not Medicare, Medicaid or some other public program) health insurance coverage.

And it will likely have relatively little impact on those individuals who buy their own coverage in the individual market and are relatively satisfied with that coverage (which would include my wife and youngest daughter).

It may not even have much impact on the (mostly young and healthy) uninsured who live in relatively low-cost states because they already have access to affordable policies and choose not to buy them. But the Health Care Choice Act could be an enormous benefit to those individuals, most of whom are uninsured, who live in the high-cost states and have no access to an affordable policy.

V. Conclusion.

We as a society would think it very self-centered if that Cadillac dealer discussed earlier took the position that if people couldn't afford one of his Cadillacs loaded with options, they would be better off without any car. Yet that is happening to many American citizens who live in states where good intentions have lead to a lack of choice of insurers, health plans and affordability.

We are not advocating the dissolution of state regulatory authority over health insurance. We are advocating an option and health care choices for the millions of individual Americans who are currently uninsured because they can not afford all the services and "protections" prescribed by their state.

Mr. DEAL. Thank you.
Mr. De Posada.

STATEMENT OF ROBERT GARCIA de POSADA

Mr. DE POSADA. Thank you, Mr. Chairman. Thank you, Mr. Brown. My name is Robert de Posada, and I am President of The Latino Coalition.

I think most people, by now, realize that Hispanics are way more uninsured in numbers than any other ethnic group in the country. According to the U.S. Census Bureau and according to almost every study, you see Hispanics tend to be three times as likely to be uninsured, and predominantly, that is based on the source of employment and their income.

In most cases, we are seeing Hispanics working for small businesses and earning a much lower income, which has put them in a very awkward situation, in being outside of a current system. Most Hispanics will be outside of the employer-based market.

When you start looking at some of the States where Hispanics are predominant, you see in these situations, Hispanics tend to live in States that are heavily mandated and that you have very serious mandates; and their premiums are extremely high.

I mean, I have been listening to Mr. Pallone when he talks. In New Jersey, it is a little more expensive—no, it is 10 times more expensive than in neighboring Pennsylvania. So we cannot, you know, we are already seeing people from New Jersey going to Pennsylvania to see people purchase insurance.

Somehow, I just don't understand how people could be supportive right now of reimportation of drugs from other countries yet have a serious concern over buying insurance across State lines.

I live in Washington State and I am lucky enough to have a good State insurance commissioner that, under his leadership, we have actually seen improvement.

I mean, in 1999, there was only one provider. Right now, we have about eight providers, but still there is no competition. We still have 84 percent of the consumers under two plans. I personally have uninsured trying to purchase insurance, I can purchase insurance in Virginia three times cheaper—the same insurance, three times cheaper than I can buy in my home State.

So I think the whole concept of allowing people to have more choices—you know, if you live in New Jersey, you have that ability to go to Pennsylvania. But if you live in south Florida, if you live in south Texas, if you live in east L.A., you are stuck. You have absolutely no options.

I think for anybody to tell me that if there is a history of diabetes in my family, that I am just going to go for the cheaper insurance and not look for insurance that would target my potential diseases. I think they are underestimating the intelligence of the consumer.

Hispanics are desperately, right now, looking for opportunities, looking for options and choices to be able to have some basic coverage. That is what we don't have right now. In every single survey, every single poll that we have conducted shows affordability is the No. 1 issue for Hispanics.

We tested this legislation late last year, and we found that 84 percent of Hispanics strongly supported the concept of this legislation, and 80 percent of Hispanics said they actually would purchase health insurance in another State if it was appropriate for them. So I think that you have a very strong level of support out there for some new alternatives, some new thinking outside of a box.

You know, at first, to be quite honest, when we were approached about this legislation, we have serious concern because there is a lot of predators in the Hispanic community. When we saw the plans available under this legislation would have to be approved by the State insurance commissioner and they would be regulated by a State, at least that gives us the peace of mind that we are going to find something that is not predatory, that is, something that will provide choices to most of the uninsured Hispanics; and I think it would give us the ability to start educating the community into the ability of getting new options for them and being able to reduce that unacceptable level of uninsured that we have in the Hispanic community.

So thank you very much, Mr. Chairman.

[The prepared statement of Robert Garcia de Posada follows:]

PREPARED STATEMENT OF ROBERT GARCIA DE POSADA, PRESIDENT, THE LATINO COALITION

My name is Robert Garcia de Posada and I am the President of The Latino Coalition. The Latino Coalition was established in 1995 to address policy issues that directly affect the well-being of Hispanics in the U.S. The Coalition's agenda is to develop and promote policies that will enhance overall business, economic and social development of Hispanics.

When it comes to health insurance, according to the U.S. Census Bureau, the highest uninsured rate in the U.S. is among people of Hispanic origin. Over one third, or 34.2% of Hispanics were uninsured compared with only 12% for non-Hispanic whites. U.S. Hispanics also have the largest percentage of the working uninsured at 37.9% compared to only 14.9% for non-Hispanic whites. Foreign-born immigrants were even worse off with more than half without health insurance. According to the Commonwealth Fund, in small- to medium-sized companies with fewer than 100 workers, 63 percent of white workers have health benefits compared with 38 percent of Hispanic workers.

There is a strong relationship between un-insurance and the kind of employment a person has. The reason is simple: Most Americans get their health insurance through their place of work. Moreover, in getting their health insurance through the workplace, they are also eligible to get large and, under current law, unlimited federal tax breaks for the purchase of health insurance. There is no such tax relief for workers who get health insurance outside the workplace or for workers and their families who cannot get employer-based health insurance.

Today, 65 percent of the uninsured are in working families where the breadwinner works full time. Because Hispanic workers are heavily concentrated in the service industry and in small businesses—working for firms that do not or cannot offer them health insurance coverage—they are disproportionately found outside of the normal channels of health insurance in the United States.

The health insurance market in the United States is uniquely job based. All Americans, both employers and employees, get tax relief if and only if they get their health insurance coverage through their place of employment. If the employer offers health insurance, the employer gets unlimited tax relief in the form of a tax deduction as part of the cost of doing business. Likewise, under this arrangement, employees also get unlimited tax relief for purchasing health insurance through their employer. But, instead of a tax deduction, an employee gets what is technically called a "tax exclusion" on the value of the job's health benefits. Self employed individuals also receive their health insurance tax-free. So the people who are left out of the tax-free world of health benefits are people who have to buy their own individual plan; indeed, the federal tax code punishes workers who buy health insurance outside the workplace by making that worker buy health benefits with after-tax dollars. For most workers, this cost is a huge disincentive for obtaining health insurance on their own.

The main reasons so many Hispanics do not have health insurance are they generally have lower incomes and they work for smaller firms. Employment and income level are the leading indicators of health insurance coverage in this country. The lower the income, the more likely a worker will not have coverage. If they are working independently or with a firm that does not provide health insurance, they simply do not have coverage because they cannot afford it. Small firms, with fewer than 25 employees, are the least likely to provide employment-based health insurance. Based on the 1990 Census, odds are that Hispanic workers—with a per capita income of only $10,773 and a solid majority employed by small businesses, particularly the service industry—will not be offered health insurance at the workplace and will not be able to afford it on their own.

Low-skilled workers often do not work for large companies or command a wage that enables them to buy health insurance, and they get little if any government assistance in purchasing it. If a worker decides to purchase individual policies, they will soon realize it is prohibitively expensive. This is the problem facing America's working poor.

Since most Latinos have to buy their own health insurance, they are faced with many obstacles to an affordable plan. All too often, state lawmakers have passed laws that require us to pay for benefits we may not want or need. While well intentioned, these mandates increase the cost of health insurance and push it beyond our means.

And that's the main reason we strongly support H.R. 2355, the "Health Care Choice Act."

H.R. 2355 will be a great tool for many of these uninsured workers to have access to more affordable health insurance plans. This legislation will open the doors to affordable coverage for all uninsured Hispanics and allow us to buy a health plan that meets our needs.

This bill is especially beneficial for those in the individual market. And most Hispanic workers fit that category. These are the workers who don't get the tax break like everyone else does; don't have an employer paying a significant amount of the cost; and have to buy a policy full of mandates which employers who self insure are able to escape. To add insult to injury, these workers have lower incomes, so they end up unable to afford these health insurance plans in the individual health insurance market.

This legislation will provide them with a new tool to find better plans that will fit their needs and their budgets. If you live in states with excessive mandates or with guaranteed issue and community ratings the cost of any individual plan is out of the reach of most workers. Under this legislation, workers in those states will be able to shop for plans approved by a State Insurance Commissioner in other states where the prices might be more suitable for their budgets and their particular needs.

Let me give you an example, if you are a family of four (husband and wife both age 35, two kids aged 10 and 9) living in Easton, Pennsylvania (right across the border), a health insurance plan will cost you $299.81 per month for a $1,000 deductible. That same family in New Jersey (any town because it costs the same throughout NJ because of community rating) it would cost $3,820.11 a month for a $500 deductible, according to the New Jersey Department of insurance (January 2005).

Many families in New Jersey have been buying insurance across state lines for years now. But what happens if you live in South Florida, South Texas or East Los Angeles and don't have the resources to travel across state lines? You are stuck with the very high cost insurance. This legislation will allow uninsured workers the ability to shop around for plans that meet their needs and fit their budgets.

Personally, I am a healthy individual and I am currently uninsured. I wanted to purchase an HSA in my home state of Washington State. But it's too expensive. I can purchase that same plan in Virginia for quite a bit less. Why can't someone like me be able to shop around across state lines to find plans that fit my needs and my budget? As long as it is regulated by a State Insurance Commissioner, why is the government limiting my choices?

That's why this legislation is enormously popular among Hispanics. In a survey we conducted in October 2004 among 1,000 Hispanic adults, 84 percent strongly supported allowing people to buy an insurance policy from a different state as long as the health insurance product is regulated and approved by the state. The support was consistent across all sub groups: gender, age, party affiliation, national ancestry, registered and non-registered voters, ideology, and region. And a follow-up question showed that 84 percent would buy a health insurance plan from another state, as long as the plan was regulated and approved by the state.

When we first heard the basic concept of this legislation, we had serious concerns because of the number of predators in the Hispanic market. But when we realize that the only plans available under this legislation would be plans approved by a

State Insurance Commissioner and regulated by all insurance commissioners, we realized that this concern was seriously addressed.

By no means do we believe that this is the silver bullet that will solve the uninsured crisis, but it's a great step in the right direction. This legislation, combined with 1) refundable tax credits for uninsured workers, 2) an increase in the number of community health centers, and 3) medical malpractice reform to eliminate provisions that prevent physicians from serving patients in underserved and low-income areas, among others.

The Latino Coalition strongly commends this committee for addressing this issue, and we look forward to working with you to break down the barriers and build the necessary bridges to improve the access to affordable health coverage for the uninsured.

Thank you.

Mr. DEAL. Thank you.

Mr. Kreidler.

STATEMENT OF MIKE KREIDLER

Mr. KREIDLER. Thank you, Mr. Chairman. Good morning, and thank you for all of the kind words that have been expressed by you and the committee members. My name is Mike Kreidler. I am the Washington State Insurance Commissioner, and I am here today to represent the National Association of Insurance Commissioners, the NAIC, which regulates insurance in 50 States, the District of Columbia and five U.S. territories.

Just to show that we are a very bipartisan group, I should point out that the majority, about two-thirds of the State's insurance commissioners are appointed, almost always by the Governor, and the rest are elected. The majority of our membership would be much like this body, of Republican background either by appointment or election as opposed to Democrat.

The NAIC is about consumer protection. With that in mind, I am here today to speak to the Health Care Choice Act of 2005.

We clearly share the same concerns of the committee and the sponsors of this legislation about affordability and accessibility of individual health insurance. The NAIC has been very involved, as have the States, in trying to stabilize an increasingly fragile, individual small group of markets in our respective States.

In the past 15 years, 31 States have approved high-risk pools. That helps to make sure that individuals who can't find insurance have an avenue for it. The truth is, though, that even in our State the vast majority, that are eligible for the high-risk pool and can't find other insurance, are screened in our State into the high-risk pool, but can't afford the premiums. As a consequence, it is a relatively small number that get it by virtue of participation in that pool.

While we very much support and commend the sponsor of this legislation, Representative Shadegg, for his support of both the extension and the expansion of high-risk pools which he has done in the 108th Congress, we would like to urge this body to also take up the legislation in the committee. In the U.S. Senate's committee, the appropriate committee has already done so.

Congressman Eshoo has already mentioned that States are frequently the kind of—where ideas are developed, and it is absolutely true. We are the incubators and the laboratories for new ideas, reinsurance, tax credits, subsidies, disease management, medical necessity, healthy lifestyles. All are issues that are being worked at the State level.

Now, we have some concerns about the Health Care Choice Act. I need to express those. Our concern—well, wanting to work with the sponsor of this legislation, we see some serious risks here, disadvantages to high-risk individuals and the preemption of critical consumer protection as a part of this legislation. Just because you have health insurance is not a guarantee that you are going to have health insurance that has value.

You wind up with adverse selection; if you need a comprehensive policy—and all those that need it go there, and those that don't need it, don't—you find that policy unaffordable. Or it goes out of business, either as a product that is offered or the company that is offering it. We need to make sure that we don't wind up fragmenting health care any worse than it already is, separating the healthier and younger from the less well and older; and this legislation would have that impact.

Health care is very expensive in some States. We in Washington State would very much like to have the Medicare reimbursement of New Jersey and New York. We are far from that. So would California, I am sure. We are afraid that this is going to be a race to the bottom from the standpoint that the States that do offer health insurance are going to be those with the least regulation, are going to be those with the least resources to aid consumers, and we as States being preempted from our authority, being able to intervene for consumers, are going to be left not able to represent them.

We will also find that there is going to be a disadvantage to our State and our regional health insurers who are going to wind up in a position of not having to compete with national insurers that are offering very weak products and rate deregulated.

The real issue is, how do we balance the interests of the consumers, how do we make sure that we have the ability through licensing of our health insurers to make sure that they are, in fact, living up to the full efforts of the law?

Thank you, Mr. Chairman. I look forward to your questions.

[The prepared statement of Mike Kreidler follows:]

PREPARED STATEMENT OF HON. MIKE KREIDLER, COMMISSIONER, WASHINGTON STATE OFFICE OF INSURANCE, ON BEHALF OF THE NATIONAL ASSOCIATION OF INSURANCE COMMISSIONERS

INTRODUCTION

Good morning Mister Chairman. My name is Mike Kreidler, Commissioner of the Washington State Office of Insurance. I am testifying today on behalf of the National Association of Insurance Commissioners (NAIC). The NAIC represents the chief insurance regulators from the 50 States, the District of Columbia, and five U.S. territories. The primary objective of insurance regulators is to protect consumers and it is with this goal in mind that I comment today generally on the current uninsured crisis, and in particular the "Health Care Choice Act of 2005."

To begin, I will emphasize the commissioners' recognition of how important it is to ensure affordable, available health coverage for all Americans and offer the full support of the NAIC in developing legislation that will reach these goals. States have acted aggressively over the past fifteen years to stabilize and improve the individual health insurance market. Most notably, thirty-one States have created high-risk pools, providing a safety net for over 170,000 people with chronic illnesses and other pre-existing conditions. The State high-risk pools collect almost $650 million pear year in premiums and pay over $1 billion in claims. This subsidized coverage has proven critical to individuals and families with high medical expenses and to the stability of the individual health insurance market.

As an aside, the NAIC continues to support legislation at the federal level that would expand and extend the high-risk pool grants created in the Trade Act of 2002. We applaud Representative Shadegg for introducing such a bill in the 108th Congress. The Senate Health, Education, Labor and Pensions Committee has already acted this year on legislation—we encourage the House act soon on what has become an important subsidy for high-risk individuals.

States continue to experiment with other strategies for making health insurance more affordable for individuals, including: reinsurance, tax credits, subsidies, basic health plans, and programs to promote healthier lifestyles and manage diseases. As always, States are the laboratories for innovative ideas. It is critical that the federal government and the States work closely with healthcare providers, insurers and consumers to implement true reforms that will curb spending and make insurance more affordable.

CONCERNS ABOUT THE HEALTH CARE CHOICE ACT

The nation's health insurance regulators cannot support federal legislation that would disadvantage higher-risk individuals or preempt critical consumer protections. This is why the NAIC opposes Association Health Plan legislation and why we do not support the Health Care Choice Act of 2005, H.R. 2355. While we appreciate attempts by the author to preserve some level of State oversight, we must emphasize that it is poor public policy to allow the sale of health insurance in a State without oversight of the resident regulator. Such a policy is an open invitation to fraud and abuse.

As currently drafted, H.R. 2355 would allow an insurance company to choose a single State in which to license its individual health insurance product and then sell it in any other State, avoiding that State's laws and regulations. This would clearly promote a "race to the bottom" as insurers would be greatly rewarded for licensing their individual products in States with less regulation and fewer personnel to oversee what could be a large influx of new products.

State insurance commissioners acknowledge there are many challenges facing the individual health insurance market. In response, many States have adopted NAIC model laws that provide strong consumer protection and product standards that ensure consumers receive value for premiums paid. Unfortunately, not all States have adopted these models. Therefore, we are concerned that health insurers will seek those States with lower standards for their product approvals. In essence, this bill would undermine efforts by States to improve insurance coverage. Speed to market is important, but valueless products do more harm to consumers and the market overall.

For example, most States have enacted laws limiting preexisting condition exclusions. Many States have implemented rating limits to ensure the higher costs of sicker consumers are spread across the population. Some States have created reinsurance mechanisms to spread the risk among insurers. States have also enacted important consumer protections to ensure access to providers. H.R. 2355 would undermine all of these protections, wiping out any progress that has been made on behalf of consumers.

In addition, if H.R. 2355 were enacted State regulators would be unable to assist their own constituents, leaving consumers to seek assistance from the insurer's home State. While that may be a theoretical possibility, in the real world of tight State budgets it will be virtually impossible to assist a nonresident consumer in a distant State. And the home State of the consumer will be unable to assist, as it has no jurisdiction over a company not licensed in the State. Also, the fragile individual health insurance market would be disrupted, as properly licensed insurance companies would be forced to compete on an unlevel playing field. Specifically, small and regional insurers would be disadvantaged by large national companies entering States with inferior products and unregulated rates.

While we understand the desire of the bill's supporters to make health insurance more accessible to individuals, we remain concerned that this bill would do great harm to those who need insurance the most and would leave many consumers without assistance when they need it most. Unlike group insurance consumers, individuals shopping for coverage do not have the sophistication of an employer when making coverage decisions. Consumers in the individual market need the protections afforded by State regulation.

NAIC'S PRINCIPLES FOR FEDERAL REFORM

In their search for effective solutions, the nation's insurance regulators have identified seven basic principles by which federal health insurance reform legislation can be analyzed. These principles are intended to keep the focus on the needs of consumers and the true causes of the current crisis. These principles are:

Principle 1: The rights of all consumers must be protected. States already have patient protections, solvency standards, fraud prevention programs, and oversight mechanisms in place to protect consumers; unless new federal standards equal or exceed existing State standards and enforcement they should not be preempted. Any new insurance arrangement purporting to increase the number of people with health insurance will be a failure if the insurance arrangement is not solvent and cannot pay the claims of those who have placed their trust in it. Further, all new proposals must preserve access to sufficient grievance and appeals procedures, and also assure that benefits and provider networks are adequate. Consumers must always be protected from fraud and misinformation.

Principle 2: Existing State reforms and assistance programs must be supported, not degraded. As you know, States have already enacted small group purchasing pools, high-risk pools, and other reforms to increase the availability and affordability of health insurance. Federal reforms must not erode these successful efforts by permitting good risk to be siphoned off through manipulation of benefit design or eligibility for benefit provisions.

Principle 3: Adequate consumer education must be provided. Federal reform will be complicated, creating new insurance choices for many Americans. The federal government must coordinate with existing State consumer education programs to ensure consumers are able to make informed choices.

Principle 4: The overarching issue of rising healthcare costs must be addressed. Federal efforts to increase access to insurance will not be successful over time unless the overriding issue of rapidly rising healthcare costs is also addressed. Insurance is a mechanism for paying for health care and has had only limited success in controlling costs, but insurance is not the cause of those skyrocketing costs. There are multiple drivers of healthcare costs, and they in turn are driving up the cost of health insurance. To bring long-term stability to the healthcare system efforts must include provisions to address cost drivers and control rising healthcare costs.

Principle 5. Current cost shifting must not be exacerbated. Inadequate reimbursement payments have led to cost shifting to the private sector. Unfunded federal mandates to States have shifted costs onto State governments. The cost of providing care to the uninsured is also shifted, driving up rates for insurance consumers. These actions have resulted in higher overall costs and decreased access for many consumers. Federal health insurance reform legislation must address cost shifting.

Principle 6: The position of less healthy individuals must be protected. Both State and the federal governments have begun the process of reforming tax structure and other financial policies to encourage individuals to be more responsible consumers of health care. Emerging industry trends reflect developments in benefit and plan designs that create incentives for responsible consumer behavior in health care purchasing decisions. Public policy decisions must assure that new designs do not shift costs to such an extent that insurance no longer offers meaningful protection to the sick or discourage appropriate care. Federal legislation should encourage appropriate usage of the health care system without inappropriately withholding needed health care services to the sicker patient.

Principle 7: Public policymakers should be wary of allowing the creation of insurance companies without appropriate oversight. Remember, legislation that allows alternative risk-bearing arrangements must acknowledge that it is allowing the creation of new insurance companies. A mere change in the name of the arrangement does not transform its essential insurance nature and function—the acceptance and spreading of risk. To allow such new insurance companies to be formed outside the existing regulatory structure will create an unlevel playing field that is unfair to existing insurers and potentially harmful to consumers. To do so without providing adequate additional federal resources to ensure sufficient oversight of new entities will be disastrous.

ALTERNATIVES FOR REAL REFORM

As mentioned earlier, States are experimenting with a variety of strategies for reducing the number of uninsured. A majority of States have created high-risk pools to assist "uninsurable" individuals. Several States are utilizing reinsurance mechanisms, with various degrees of success. The most recent effort by the State of New

York in its Healthy New York program has used a retrospective reinsurance mechanism, subsidized by State tax dollars, that has resulted in about 70,000 new insureds, all low wage workers who were formerly uninsured.

As another example, in Maine, the State enacted the Dirigo Health Plan, intended to provide coverage for 180,000 State residents. The plan has two components: 1) expansion of Medicaid and SCHIP to parents with incomes up to 200% of the federal poverty line and to everyone earning less than 125% of the federal poverty line; and 2) establishment of a public/private plan to cover business with 2-50 employees, the self-employed, and unemployed and part-time workers. The plan is in its early stages of implementation, and State policymakers have high hopes for its success.

All of these reforms have been carefully crafted, weighing the needs of all populations and preserving key consumer protections. The federal government should look to these and other State programs for possible solutions to the uninsured crisis, not proposals that sweep aside State innovations and reforms in favor of injurious federal policies.

CONCLUSION

All of us recognize that it is very important to make health insurance available all Americans. The States have begun to address this problem, and will continue to do so. However, the problem is complex and does not lend itself to easy solutions.

The federal government and the States need to work with healthcare providers, insurers and consumers to implement true reforms that will curb spending and make insurance more affordable. We stand ready to work with members of Congress to draft effective reforms that will address both the affordability and availability issues facing individuals. Together, real solutions to this critical issue can be found.

Mr. DEAL. Thank you.

Mr. Limbaugh.

STATEMENT OF L. HUNTER LIMBAUGH

Mr. LIMBAUGH. Mr. Chairman and members of the committee, thank you for the opportunity to speak to you today. I am Hunter Limbaugh, volunteer chairman of the American Diabetes Association's national advocacy committee. More important to me, I am the father of an incredible, beautiful and brilliant, and exasperating 10-year-old little girl, who was diagnosed with diabetes at the age of 6.

We are facing a crisis in this country. The diabetes epidemic is one that, regrettably, I don't believe Congress has yet come to terms with. There are 18.2 million Americans with diabetes, and every year there are an additional 1.5 million people diagnosed with the disease. That extrapolates or interpolates, one or the other, to about 42,000 per congressional district.

Next time you are at a function in your district and look around the room, it is safe to say that about half the people there either have diabetes, or their mother, father, sister, brother or child has it. The CDC says one-third of Americans born will be diagnosed with diabetes at some point in their lives.

In our minority communities, the incidence is even higher; in fact, our Latino Diabetes Action Council recently toured the South Texas border region. In Starr County, where the population is essentially 100 per Latino, 30 percent of the population has diabetes; and they have the highest incidence of lower limb amputation in the country.

The human, societal and financial cost of these numbers is, or ought to be, shocking. To illustrate the financial cost of the disease, let me remind you that diabetes costs this country $132 billion per year, and that number will grow commensurate with the growth of the disease.

Unfortunately, the fact that you are seriously considering legislation, H.R. 2355, the Health Care Choice Act, that would likely undermine efforts to manage and mitigate these costs suggests that Congress has yet to fully understand the scope and nature of the diabetes crisis in America. The days when my daughter's diagnosis would likely have consigned her to a greatly reduced length and quality of life likely to have included complications such as kidney disease, blindness, lower limb amputation, heart disease, et cetera, should be behind us. It is now possible for people to manage diabetes in such a way as to greatly reduce the chances of developing the complications I just mentioned.

It has been definitively proven that failure to adequately control the disease results in a 50 percent increase in the likelihood of developing those serious complications. However, in order to do what is necessary to control the disease, people with diabetes must have access to adequate health insurance coverage. I emphasize the word here "adequate."

As has already been mentioned, adequacy is at least as important as accessibility. I would analogize it to, I can afford to buy a car, but if that car breaks down halfway to work every day in the worst most crime-ridden part of town, I have got a car, but the darned thing is going to get me killed one of these days; so I am not sure I am any better off.

It is for that reason that the association has spent the past 10 years convincing legislatures and Governors of both parties in 46 States of the need for mandated diabetes coverage in insurance policies. In fact, former Governor and HSS Secretary, Tommy Thompson, was the first to sign one in 1991.It exists in Georgia. It exists in Arizona. It exists in my State of South Carolina.

As a former Republican legislator myself, I have to say I am very troubled by the notion that Congress should be substituting its judgment in this area for that of the legislatures of 46 States. I can assure you that the notion that diabetes mandates are responsible for increasing the cost of insurance is simply wrong.

Numerous States have studied the costs of these mandates and concluded that their costs are de minimis. For example, Louisiana determined that the diabetes mandate accounted for six one-thousandths of 1 percent of the monthly premium. Utah, after a similar analysis, satisfied itself that there was no cost at all and strengthened its mandate.

The danger inherent in H.R. 2355, however well intentioned it may be—and I am sure is—is that insurers will be free to domicile in one of the four States that do not have a diabetes mandate, thereby undermining the will of the 46 States that have determined that such a mandate is in the best interests of their citizens. The ability of Americans to manage their diabetes will be greatly eroded to their personal detriment and to the detriment of the country as a whole.

This is a time when we need to be exploring options for expanding coverage for people with diabetes. It is past time to be treating diabetes as the human health care and financial crisis that it manifestly is. Giving people the tools to manage their diabetes, the most important of which is adequate insurance coverage, must be our focus; and the American Diabetes Association continues to stand ready to work with you to achieve that.

Thank you for your time, and I am happy to try to answer any questions you may have.

[The prepared statement of L. Hunter Limbaugh follows:]

American Diabetes Association.

Mission • To prevent and cure diabetes and to improve the lives of all people affected by diabetes.

Cure • Care • Commitment™

Statement of

L. Hunter Limbaugh
Chairman, National Advocacy Committee
American Diabetes Association

To the United States House of Representatives Committee on Energy and Commerce
Subcommittee on Health

Hearing on H.R. 2355, the "Health Care Choice Act"

June 28, 2005

Mr. Chairman and members of the Committee, on behalf of the 18.2 million Americans living with diabetes and the more than 40 million living with pre-diabetes, I would like to thank you for the opportunity to appear before you today on this very important issue. My name is Hunter Limbaugh and I am chairman of the American Diabetes Association's National Advocacy Committee and the father of an amazing little girl who has lived with diabetes for 4 years.

Like Members of this Committee, the Association is committed to expanding and improving health insurance coverage. The Association maintains that people with diabetes should have access to affordable and adequate health insurance, such as coverage for blood glucose monitoring and related supplies, insulin and delivery mechanisms such as syringes and/or pumps, prescribed oral medications for controlling blood sugar, diabetes education at regular intervals, and podiatric services and supplies. We have secured state laws that provide this coverage in 46 states and the District of Columbia. Our understanding of H.R. 2355, the "Health Care Choice Act," is that it would allow health insurers to pick any state from which to operate from and then sell health plans across state lines, potentially by-passing the state laws. While we recognize that one goal of this bill is to provide greater choice to those seeking health insurance, upon reviewing the legislation, we are deeply concerned about the negative impact it would have on people with diabetes.

As the nation's leading nonprofit health organization providing diabetes research, information and advocacy, the Association has a significant interest in reducing the number of uninsured and underinsured in the United States. As you probably are aware, diabetes is a serious, life-threatening, chronic illness for which there is no cure. *Approximately 42,000 people suffering from diabetes live in each congressional district and that number is growing by an estimated 8% per year.* In fact, current estimates by the Centers for Disease Control and Prevention reflect that one of every three children born in the U.S. after 2000 will develop diabetes in their lifetime. For minorities, that number increase to one in every two children. While we do not have a cure for the disease, the disease can be successfully managed with access to the necessary tools.

For people with diabetes, it is simply not true that having any health insurance is better than having no health insurance. Having access to adequate health insurance coverage is as this country's best interest to ensure that people with diabetes are receiving the preventive care they need. Failing to do so will have disastrous economic effects.

Why is diabetes management so important? Scientific studies have proven time and time again that inadequate control increases the risk of diabetes complications by more than 50%. If insurers provide only limited health coverage that excludes preventive coverage for diabetes, we absolutely guarantee that this nation will see even more exorbitant diabetes-related expenses in the future. As more Americans develop diabetes and fewer have adequate insurance, the current national cost of $132 billion per year will be dwarfed with every passing year. If we allow the cost of diabetes to escalate at the same rate as the disease itself, 8% annually, we will be subtracting at least another $10 billion from the national economy every year –and this does not account for the ever-increasing cost of health care. Recently, the Association's Latino Diabetes Action Council toured the South Texas border region. Starr County, a county that is comprised literally of 100% Latinos, is a perfect example of what we are talking about: with 30% of the population living with diabetes, compared to the national average for Latinos of 11.3%, it suffers also from the highest rate of lower limb amputations. This is clearly a population that would not benefit from a pared-down insurance plan with no or limited coverage for diabetes care and supplies. Again, I reiterate that we cannot fall into the trap of taking a short-term economic view of this disease. The bottom line is that it is in this country's best interest to expand the number of people with diabetes who are receiving the care they need to prevent complications. Reducing coverage will have disastrous economic effects.

Although the economic cost is an important argument, we should not ignore the impact of diabetic complications on the quality of life of every individual with the disease. Do we want to create a future which guarantees blindness, amputation, heart disease, stroke and kidney failure for people with diabetes? If the federal government facilitates the reduction of diabetes benefits, we will be committing a tragedy of epic proportions. Through research paid by tax dollars and grants from the Association and other entities, we have learned a great deal about how to treat and manage this disease. However, this knowledge will be wasted if individuals will be unable to afford the tools they need, and insurers will refuse to pay for those tools. Abetted by the federal government, insurers will take only a short-term view, thus assuring debilitating consequences for people with diabetes.

We need a health care and health insurance system that helps diabetes patients to manage their care; we cannot afford –either in economic or moral terms– to implement a system which makes it more difficult. H.R. 2355, unfortunately, would do the latter instead of the former. By allowing all insurers to be domiciled in states without state diabetes requirements, minimum-coverage plans would become the norm across the country: thus will begin the deadly domino effect that will harm all people with diabetes who currently have proper insurance coverage for their needs.

One of the biggest tragedies of this bill –and the actions of insurers– is that it is based on misconceptions. Some have expressed a view that diabetes requirements are costly for insurers and the health care system. However, numerous states have studied the cost of diabetes benefit laws and have found that the impact on overall health costs is insignificant. Louisiana, for example, found that their state diabetes requirement accounted for a mere .006% of monthly premiums.[1] In Utah, after a similar analysis,[2] legislators chose to strengthen their state law after finding that the added cost of the diabetes requirement was non-existent. I urge you to not pass a bill that is so clearly based on misperception.

Just as important as overall statistics and abstraction, however, is the real-life impact that inadequate insurance has on people with diabetes. In conjunction with Georgetown University, the Association recently compiled a study to address this topic entitled "*Falling Through the Cracks: Stories of How Health Insurance Can Fail People With Diabetes,*" which shows what happens to people with diabetes when they do not have access to adequate *and* affordable insurance coverage.

During this research, we came across many Americans who had exhausted all of their health insurance options and had nowhere left to turn. For example, we spoke to Joanne, a woman from Ohio, one of the four states without diabetes insurance requirements. Joanne's case demonstrates the need for protecting the existing state laws and allowing other states to do the same: Joanne has health insurance, but it does not cover her diabetes supplies. Specifically, it

[1] *Louisiana Department of Insurance.* A Study of the Costs Associated with Healthcare Benefits Mandated in Louisiana. February 28, 2003.
[2] *Utah Insurance Department.* 2003 Diabetes Mandate Report, October 28, 2003.

does not cover her test strips, which cost $160 per month. For people with diabetes, avoidance of serious complications, like those mentioned previously, depends on constant monitoring of their blood sugar levels. It is therefore essential that people with diabetes have access to a sufficient quantity of test strips. In addition to the cost of her test strips, Joanne pays about $200 per month for her out of pocket portion for her diabetes medications. She does not qualify for pharmaceutical assistance programs since she is insured. Many months, Joanne has been forced to choose between taking care of her health by purchasing test strips, or having heat in the house during the winter. If, under H.R. 2355, insurers choose to be domiciled in a state that does not require policies to include diabetes supplies and education, we could have tens of thousands of Joanns in all 50 states, instead of just four.

Each of the examples highlighted in our report underscores the need for diabetes patients to have health insurance coverage that meets three key components: availability, affordability and adequacy. For people with diabetes, having inadequate health insurance – even if considered "affordable"– may, in fact, be worse that having no insurance because they are then required to pay health insurance premiums in addition non-reimbursed out-of-pocket costs for their life-sustaining diabetes supplies and medications. As such, poor-quality insurance actually steals critical resources from families affected by diabetes while providing nothing in return except catastrophic protection. Many patients in this type of situation are forced to ration their test strips – leading to glucose testing several times per month instead of several times per day. Less knowledge about their glucose levels leads to poor control, which in turn guarantees a diabetes-related hospitalization. In an ironic and destructive turn of events, inadequate health insurance in year 1 provides no coverage for preventive medicine, which then guarantees a much higher-cost catastrophic hospitalization in year 5.

This never ending cycle also forces many people with diabetes and other chronic disease into bankruptcy. In fact, the *New York University Law Review* found that medical bills are the single leading factor contributing to personal bankruptcy in the U.S.[3] Moreover, two-thirds of these bankruptcies occurred in people who *had health insurance coverage*.

[3] *Jacoby, M. B., Sullivan, T. A. and Warren, E.*, Rethinking the Debates over Health Care Financing: Evidence from the Bankruptcy Courts. New York University Law Review, Volume 76, Number 2, May 2001: 375 – 415

We are facing a diabetes crisis in this country and simply cannot facilitate the creation of poor health insurance options for people with diabetes. Cutting them off from necessary medical tools will only increase the number of debilitating and expensive complications, leading to even higher societal costs. The Association shares your concern in increasing access to health insurance coverage, but we strongly believe that a bill that negatively impacts the health of people with diabetes is not the answer.

In conclusion, please be aware that the Association is also working on positive solutions to our health care crisis. As stated above, significant evidence shows that proper diabetes care in the short-term dramatically reduces complications and costs in the long-term. Therefore, the Association's guiding principle for health care reform is that it must be focused on transforming our system from a model of crisis care to a model of preventive care. While the Association cannot support H.R. 2355, we stand ready to work with you to address the problems individuals, including those with chronic illnesses such as diabetes, face in accessing affordable and adequate health care coverage.

Thank you. I am happy to answer any questions you may have.

Mr. DEAL. Thank you.
Dr. Gratzer.

STATEMENT OF DAVID GRATZER

Mr. GRATZER. Thank you, Mr. Chairman.

Thank you, Mr. Chairman, members of the committee—subcommittee. I am honored to testify today on these hearings on the Health Care Choice Act before the Committee on Energy and Commerce Subcommittee on Health.

My name is David Gratzer. I am a physician and a Senior Fellow at the Manhattan Institute in New York City. The views I present today are my own and do not necessarily represent those of The Manhattan Institute.

As many of you are well aware, insurance premiums vary greatly State to State. eHealthInsurance, leading online insurance brokerage, recently compared the cost of a standard family insurance policy, $2,000 deductible, 20 percent coinsurance across the Nation's 50 largest cities. That comparison involved some 4,000 insurance plans and 140 insurance companies.

The results are startling. Consider a nonemployer-based policy for a family of four in Kansas City, Missouri, costs about $170 a month, while similar coverage in Boston tops more than $750 a month. In my written statement, you can see a table which illustrates the broad range of pricing.

Why the price difference? Many States dictate the type of services and providers. New York, for instance, requires that the services of a podiatrist be covered. Now, as you know, it is a commonly quoted statistic that the average person walks about a 150,000 miles in a lifetime. And I am hoping that the majority of your journey, Mr. Chairman, is on healthy, bunion-free feet. But should every insurance policy in the Empire State really be required to include the services of a podiatrist? Acupuncturists are mandated in a full 11 States; massage therapists, as Congressman Shadegg pointed out, in four; osteopaths in 24; chiropractors in 47. Each of these mandated providers drives up the price of even the most basic insurance plan.

Now, as I am sure you are aware, some States have gone much further. Laws force insurers to sell to any applicant, guaranteed issue, at the same price regardless of age or health, community rating. Faced with higher premiums for insurance they seldom use, the young and healthy drop their coverage, leaving an insurance pool of older, sicker people, and even higher premiums. After a decade of such political meddling, the average monthly cost of a family policy in New Jersey bests, frankly, the monthly lease of a Ferrari.

In such an environment, many insurance carriers choose not to do business. In Vermont, for example, just three companies sell to the individual market.

What are the consequences of the regulatory burden? I think there are three. Let me go through each one.

Higher premiums: The regulatory burden means, in effect, massive health tax for citizens in dozens of States. This hidden tax unfairly discriminates against the self-employed as well as small and medium-size businesses. Large corporations, after all, aren't forced to follow State mandates since many—in fact, most—self-insure. As you are aware, some spend more than two-thirds less than the national average for the healthy employee by using no frills plans.

Another consequence is that we have more uninsured Americans. It makes sense that the higher the premium, the more people will opt out of buying insurance. The Congressional Budget Office looked at the data and estimated for every 1 percent increase in the cost of insurance, roughly 200,000 to 300,000 more Americans are uninsured. David Cutler has subsequently gone back and his figures are a little bit more conservative at 150,000, but it is still a great number of Americans.

And the third consequence is reduced labor mobility. In a recent study University of Wisconsin economist Scott Adams demonstrates that 20 to 30 percent of nonelderly men choose to stay put a job with health benefits. No wonder, since potential employers may not offer insurance and individual policies are so pricey, particularly in cities like New York and Boston, labor mobility suffers as does American entrepreneurship.

A remedy? Allow out-of-State purchasers of health insurance, as the Health Care Choice Act proposes. The Federal McCarran-Ferguson Act of 1945 empowers States to regulate the business of insurance, quote, unquote, but nothing, however, prevents Congress from allowing interstate sales.

The foundation of such a bill would be the Constitution's commerce clause; individuals would then be able to shop around and find a low-cost policy, if they chose, an affirmation of free market principles since interstate regulations now leave many Americans at the mercy of a small number of local health insurance carriers.

Allowing a competitive market for health insurance would be a major budgetary expense, but it may prove priceless to the cause of advancing market reforms to better American health care.

Let's be clear. The Health Care Choice Act will not singlehandedly correct the problems of American health care. It does, however, Mr. Chairman represent a step in the right direction.

[The prepared statement of David Gratzer follows:]

PREPARED STATEMENT OF DAVID GRATZER, MANHATTAN INSTITUTE

I am honored to testify today in these hearings on "The Health Care Choice Act" before the Committee on Energy and Commerce's Subcommittee on Health. My name is David Gratzer. I am a physician and a senior fellow at the Manhattan Institute in New York. I'm speaking today in support of Congressman Shadegg's efforts. The views I present are my own and do not necessarily represent those of the Manhattan Institute.

As you may know, insurance premiums vary greatly from state to state. eHealthInsurance, a leading online insurance brokerage, recently compared the cost of a standard family insurance policy ($2,000 deductible with a 20% co-insurance) across the nation's 50 largest cities, involving some 4,000 insurance plans and 140 insurance companies. The results are startling. Consider: a non-employer-based family policy for four in Kansas City, Mo., costs about $170 per month while similar coverage in Boston tops more than $750 a month. (Please see the accompanying table, which further illustrates the range.)

Why the price difference? Many states dictate the type of services and providers. New York, for instance, requires that the services of a podiatrist be covered. It's a commonly quoted statistic that the average person walks about 150,000 miles in a lifetime. Let's hope the majority of this journey is on healthy, bunion-free feet. But should every insurance policy in the Empire State really be required to include podiatric services? Acupuncturists are mandated in 11 states, massage therapists in 4, osteopaths in 24, and chiropractors in 47, driving up the price of even the most basic insurance plans.

Some states have gone further. Laws force insurers to sell to any applicant (guaranteed issue) and at the same price, regardless of age or health (community rating). Faced with higher premiums for insurance they seldom use, the young and healthy drop their coverage, leaving an insurance pool of older, sicker people—and even higher premiums. After a decade of such political meddling, the average monthly cost of a family policy in New Jersey bests the monthly lease of a Ferrari. In such an environment, many insurance carriers choose not to do business; in Vermont, for example, just three companies sell to the individual market.

The consequences:

- **Higher premiums.** The regulatory burden means, in effect, a massive health tax for citizens in dozens of states. This hidden tax unfairly discriminates against the self-employed, as well as small and mid-sized companies. Large corporations, after all, aren't forced to follow state mandates (many self-insure); some spend two-thirds less than the national average on heath coverage per employee by using no-frills plans.
- **More uninsured.** It makes sense that the higher the premium, the more people will opt out of buying insurance. The CBO estimates that every 1% increase in insurance cost results in 200,000 to 300,000 more uninsured.
- **Reduced labor mobility.** In a recent study, University of Wisconsin economist Scott Adams demonstrates that 20% to 30% of non-elderly men choose to stay put at jobs with health benefits. No wonder: Since potential employers may not offer insurance and individual policies are so pricey (especially in cities like New York and Boston), labor mobility suffers, as does American entrepreneurship.

A remedy? Allow out-of-state purchases of health insurance, as the Health Care Choice Act proposes. The federal McCarran-Ferguson Act of 1945 empowers states to regulate "the business of insurance." Nothing prevents Congress, however, from allowing interstate sales. The foundation of such a bill would be the Constitution's Commerce Clause. Individuals would then be able to shop around and find a low-cost policy—an affirmation of free-market principles since interstate restrictions now leave many Americans at the mercy of a small number of local health insurance carriers.

Allowing a competitive market for health insurance won't be a major budgetary expense—but it may prove priceless to the cause of advancing market reforms to better American health care.

Let's be clear: the Health Care Choice Act will not single-handedly correct the problems of American medicine. It does, however, represent a step in the right direction.

Monthly Premiums for Family Health Insurance

Kansas City, MO	171.86
Long Beach, CA	180.00
Tuscon, AZ	184.88
Philadelphia, PA	265.80
Chicago, IL	359.01
Seattle, WA	410.00
Minneapolis, MN	529.00
New York, NY	712.77
Boston, MA	767.30

Source: eHealthInsurance

Mr. DEAL. Thank you.

I will lead off with questions, and we will follow across the committee makeup here.

Let me address one of the underlying concerns that has been expressed both in opening statements and in some of the statements of the panel today, and that is the possibility of adverse selection taking place.

I have four children. My youngest is my only unmarried, in her 20's, who is an actress and on the road all the time. She called me this week and said, Daddy, I just can't afford to renew my health insurance policy.

I think what we have currently is an adverse selection of young people who are healthy and who simply say, I can't afford the premium that it is going to cost me now. But I hear the arguments being that we will adversely select those who are the sickest and the poorest.

Now, if they are poor, they are probably going to be covered in some form or fashion under Medicaid. If they are sick, and they didn't have a health insurance policy before they got sick, they are not going to be able to buy a health insurance policy that does not exclude the illness which they have, whether it be diabetes or whatever else as a preexisting condition.

Now, aren't we already in a situation, because of the cost of health insurance, where we find that the ones who are a large portion of the uninsured are actually maybe the younger and maybe even the healthier ones; and that they are the ones who may, in fact, choose a policy that is less expensive? Am I wrong in my analysis? Would anyone care to comment?

Dr. Matthews.

Mr. MATTHEWS. Yes, sir, you are absolutely right. The young healthy individuals, those who are just out of high school, just out of college, tend to be the highest makeup, the highest percentage of the people who are uninsured. They are just getting off school, they are starting their careers, many times they are in lower income jobs, oftentimes service sector jobs that don't provide health insurance. Usually by the time they hit 30 or a little older, they have moved on into a job that is going to provide health insurance.

When New York passed its guaranteed issue legislation in 1993 or 1994, I actually got calls from students in New York who said, I have got health insurance, but this new law is going to force my premiums up so high, I can't afford them. And I am a young healthy person; of course, I have been trying to do the right thing, but I can't afford to keep my insurance. With these new premiums coming in, I am going to have to drop it.

I have no advice to offer. With the Health Care Choice Act, we would be able to have some options for them.

Mr. DEAL. Mike, you wanted to comment, but let me ask you if you would—at the same time, would you comment about your understanding of the way this legislation is drafted if a policy is written in one of the 46 States that Mr. Limbaugh alluded to that currently mandate diabetes coverage?

Is it your understanding that if this were the law, that if the policy were issued in one of those States, they would still have to comply with that mandated coverage if they were from one of those 46 States? That, plus commenting on the question I raised earlier.

Mr. KREIDLER. The answer is yes, you would be able to if all 46 mandates were equal and you had a policy that came from a company from that State, you would have then—clearly have to be approved to provide diabetic coverage.

However, you could pick one of the other four States, and as a consequence, you would have the diabetic program in those States where they were required to offer diabetes coverage, competing then with programs that say, Well, I don't have diabetes, nobody in my family does. So then you wind up gravitating with all of the people with diabetes going over to where those policies offer coverage as a consequence, because diabetes coverage is not cheap. Particularly, in certain stages, you wind up in fragile types of diabetes, you wind up with them being very expensive, and it is that dislocation of care.

It is much like maternity coverage. Not all States require and mandate maternity coverage, but if the only people who buy maternity coverage are those who are likely to have need of that coverage, it becomes cost prohibitive.

It really is a social issue. How do we balance what we wind up providing in care? It is the difference, as we have talked about: care where we are talking about younger and healthier versus less well and older. It is a balance between the two of them. And States have made the conscious decision, and some States more so than others to balance it; then you see the difference in pricing.

Mr. DEAL. Five seconds, Dr. Gratzer.

Mr. GRATZER. How old is your daughter?

Mr. DEAL. 25.

Mr. GRATZER. She is just slightly below average. The average age of the uninsured in America is about 30.

Mr. DEAL. My time is up.

Mr. Brown.

Mr. BROWN. Thank you Mr. Chairman.

Mr. Kreidler, talk to us a little bit about the incentive for insurance companies to choose to locate in States with the least amount of protection, least amount of oversight. Will that cause insurers to rush to sell products in that single State with the least possible consumer protections? Talk that through if you would.

Mr. KREIDLER. The answer is, yes, they would. If you are an insurance company, a national insurance company, and you want to sell a particular product that you couldn't get approved in many other States, you are going to seek out those with the least regulatory authority.

They are typically going to be the States with the least resources to be able to answer consumer questions. So if you are in the other 49 States and you have had this product sold from this particular State, the ability to have your consumers get answers to their questions is pretty weak because, typically, they have barely the resources to deal with their in-State residents, much less all of the inquiries that come externally. And they are the only ones that are going to deal with consumer issues.

Mr. BROWN. I would like to follow again, Mr. Kreidler—follow up again on Dr. Matthews' reference to the New York-New Jersey health insurance premiums being expensive because of numerous State mandates and legislation.

I would like, Mr. Chairman, to enter into the record a response to concerns—not specifically Dr. Matthews' statements, but to concerns that others have raised, response from Wardell Sanders, Executive Director of the New Jersey Individual Health Coverage Program board, if I could. I would like to ask you to enter that into the record.

Mr. DEAL. Without objection.

[The information referred to follows:]

healthinsuranceinfo.net
Consumer Guides

read the "News You Can Use" bulletin on this topic

Setting the Record Straight on New Jersey's Individual Health Insurance Market

by
Wardell Sanders
Executive Director
NJ Individual Health Coverage Program Board

April, 2004

[Note to Readers: This column was written in response to an article that appeared in February, 2004 in Health Care News, a publication of the Heartland Institute (an organization based in Illinois.) The publication's managing editor, Conrad Meier, wrote a highly critical and misleading case study of New Jersey's individual market regulation, but then, citing lack of space for several upcoming issues, declined to print a response by Wardell Sanders of the New Jersey Department of Banking and Insurance. In the interest of setting the record straight, healthinsuranceinfo.net is pleased to post Mr. Sanders' response in its entirety.]

The message of the article by Conrad Meier, entitled, "The New Jersey Car Wreck," in the February 2004 Health Care News, faithfully supports the stated mission of the Heartland Institute, to promote "free market" solutions to healthcare. This article is presented as a "case study," but in truth it is a polemic, and one in which some statements are incorrect and some important facts are omitted. Despite the dour portrait painted by the author, New Jersey's individual market has had some success.

Like many critics of guaranteed issuance and community rating, the article's author selected as his primary source of rate comparison the most expensive plan option available in New Jersey's individual market: Plan D with a $500 deductible. This led the author to the conclusion that New Jersey's rates are one of the highest in the nation. But are they? What if the point of comparison had been the standard HMO $30 copay plan which is available for $383.67 per month for single coverage. This plan doesn't have the usual list of exclusions found in many individual market plans and high-risk pool plans. It is a comprehensive plan that covers maternity, mental health, prescription drugs, and does not have a lifetime limit. It is available to anyone, regardless of health status, but does have a 12-month pre-existing condition exclusion. Query: How does that option stack up against other states, especially where the applicant has a health condition or is older?

The article identifies a "controversy" concerning the number of people who buy coverage in New Jersey's individual market, and cites differences in data published by the Census Bureau, Employee Benefits Research Institute, and the State. This is not a controversy; these sources are just measuring different things. Just to be clear, the State's published enrollment for the IHC Program is not intended to show total enrollment of all residents with individual coverage, just coverage through the IHC Program.

Declining enrollment in the IHC Program has been affected by the disbanding of the Health Access Program, which provided state funds to purchase IHC coverage for 23,000 covered persons. It is also affected by the increasing number of coverage options for many individuals outside the IHC Program that have become available (e.g., NJ FamilyCare, NJ KidCare, the State Health Benefits Plan for certain part-time employees, self-funded MEWAs).

Also, New Jersey's small group market has very relaxed rules for eligibility, and many individual purchasers with businesses have moved to the small group market. Eligibility for the individual market requires a lack of access to group coverage. Lower than average enrollment in New Jersey's individual market may not resemble a car wreck; it may be emblematic of the fact that people are effectively steered to less expensive group coverage. According to Census data, New Jersey has a greater percentage of its residents covered under group plans (72.1%) than the national average (65%).

The national wave of individual and small employer market regulatory reforms in the 1990s was largely in response to the failure of the free market to provide viable options to the people arguably most in need of health insurance coverage: the sick, the disabled, and older persons not eligible for Medicare. In 1992, New Jersey's largely unregulated individual market was in crisis. Carriers had increasingly developed methods for turning away business from people with any kind of health condition; the carrier of last resort was going bankrupt; and the trajectory of the market portended a collapse. The 1992 reforms helped avert the collapse of the marketplace and created some short-term stability to the market. Long-term success and viability have proven to be more difficult.

New Jersey stakeholders and policymakers have been continuing a dialogue on the proper balance of regulatory measures and market-based incentives to make the market work as well as possible. But this dialogue deserves to have an accurate and complete set of facts. The article "The New Jersey Car Wreck," needs a crash course on full disclosure.

Mr. BROWN. Mr. Kreidler, I would like you to talk about those protections that you enforce. For a lot of the public that is pretty technical. But if you could kind of run through for people not so immersed in insurance law what kinds of protections, what kinds of regulations could insurers avoid if the Shadegg bill were enacted and what that would mean for the average person and his or her health care.

Mr. KREIDLER. Thank you, Mr. Brown. We are going to take a look at a product that we have licensed in our State, which this legislation would essentially remove us from, because we wouldn't license them anymore. But we will take a look at it and make sure that they are going to—that they actually have providers that will recognize this particular health plan, that they will actually offer services under that health plan.

We are going to make sure that they have financial resources backing up that particular health insurer, which if that State is perhaps not as diligent in doing it, you have concerns that that could be a real Jeopardy question.

We don't have a guarantee fund, so it obviously means our providers and patients are going to be the ones that suffer if a company fails in another State. These are the kinds of problems that we run into.

And if the consumer comes to us and says, this company isn't doing this, it isn't providing a service that the contract calls for, that they are not paying their bills, there are some protections that have been put in the bill. But the ultimate one that gives States authority is the question, the issue of licensure. And that is what we lose essentially to a State with weak regulation of insurance.

Mr. BROWN. Thank you.

Thank you, Mr. Chairman.

Mr. DEAN. Thank the gentleman.

Mr. Shadegg.

Mr. SHADEGG. Thank you, Mr. Chairman. I thank you, Mr. Chairman. I appreciate it.

Let me begin, Mr. Matthews, with you. Minnesota has, I guess—what is the variation from highs to lows in terms of mandates by the various States?

Mr. MATTHEWS. I believe Minnesota is the highest with 62, and I think Idaho is the lowest with 13, my recollection is.

Mr. SHADEGG. Washington, DC, how many in Washington, DC?

Mr. MATTHEWS. Has relatively few, I think, so 16, 17. I would have to look at my chart here, but Washington, DC, is relatively Low.

Mr. SHADEGG. Mr. Green, I noted in his testimony, was concerned that they have a very high number of uninsured in his State, the State of Texas. Do you know how many mandates they have in the State of Texas?

Mr. MATTHEWS. I do. It is 38.

Mr. SHADEGG. Have you done an analysis or had an analysis done saying how much those mandates raise the cost of health insurance.

Mr. MATTHEWS. Yes. We have that in the chart we have available here.

We went to a group of actuaries who have been working on this area for some time, and we went down the list of the mandates. And we did an estimate of the impact of the costs.

Now, because the cost varies, the legislation varies from State to State. So you might have a mandate in one State saying that, for instance, chiropractors must be covered at the same rate as a medical doctor; another State might say, we will cover chiropractors, but only five visits a year or at 50 percent.

So they all have that same—we track it as a mandate, but it may vary from State to State. So we try to get an estimate based upon these people who do the tracking going on in the States.

The vast majority of them, we would argue, affect the cost of health insurance premium less than 1 percent. Most of them do not have a major impact. What we have tried to argue, though, is that it is the cumulation of them, when you start hitting 30 and 40 mandates, that you start adding significantly to the cost of the health insurance policy.

And interestingly, and I think your point is well taken, it would be interesting to see if people in Idaho, we just simply don't see in the newspapers people dropping dead in the streets in Idaho because they don't have as many mandates they have in Minnesota.

Mr. SHADEGG. Mr. de Posada, you made the point you think consumers can make intelligent choices; you made the strong point about diabetes.

I think the testimony of Mr. Limbaugh has been interesting on diabetes. I would note that Mr. Kreidler just said diabetes coverage is expensive. Mr. Limbaugh made a major thrust it is not that expensive. But we will put that issue aside.

Are you aware of a study by, I believe, it is My eBay that shows, when given a chance to purchase either comprehensive policies or bare bones policies, the vast percentage of people buy some form of comprehensive policy and need something in the neighborhood of 90-plus percent to buy a more comprehensive policy?

Mr. DE POSADA. Yes, absolutely, and they will—consumers will look for the product that best fits their needs. But the most important thing is what best fits their budget.

And when the chairman addressed the issue of the adverse selection, we are talking about, in my community, one out of three individuals is uninsured. If that person has diabetes, that person has absolutely no coverage, and he has no options because the cost is so prohibitive. And if they don't take care of it now with a basic plan, you know, it becomes extremely expensive as time goes on.

Mr. SHADEGG. Do you suppose they might be able to deal with a policy that didn't cover acupuncturists or massage therapists or podiatrists, as are mandated in many States?

Mr. DE POSADA. I think most people in south Arizona would agree with that.

Mr. SHADEGG. I would like to ask Mr. Gratzer, there has been testimony here about kind of the race to the bottom. Mr. Brown is deeply concerned about the race to the bottom. And Mr. Kreidler made the point that the NAIC is, if nothing else, concerned about consumer protection.

I make a pitch to Mr. Kreidler and his association that we didn't do very well with that when we passed ERISA and took the States totally out of regulating insurance. And we are not doing that with other forms that are on the table. I am trying to keep them in the business of doing some regulation, but what do you make of the case of the race to the bottom?

Mr. GRATZER. Not much.

Look, it is always a concern with regulations, getting the balance right. It is a cost/benefit analysis. I think in many States—not all States, but in many States, the pendulum has swung way too much under the auspices of consumer protection. But there is not much protection to a consumer if you can't afford a policy.

I would also point out, incidentally, where you do have competitive markets and not a lot of regulations, that policies actually tend to be more comprehensive. I think what you get rid of is the ridiculous cost differentials, like New Jersey, a family of four, having to pay more than the lease of a Ferrari for a month.

I also think in today's day and age that the best consumer protection is not regulation and not regulators, but transparency. You know, when Wendy's has a finger show up in a bit of chili in San Francisco, we know about it all across the country. Word of mouth and reputation of insurers, I think, will be the strongest protection to consumers despite what our regulator friends might suggest.

Mr. SHADEGG. Let me ask one more question, if I might, on the issue of chronic diseases such as diabetes and the issue of insurance coverage, basic coverage, or other alternatives.

Mr. GRATZER. I think that the best thing for people who suffer from chronic illness, frankly, is a health savings account. Why? Because it gives them the dollars to spend as they so choose.

The world of diabetics will soon be revolutionized. Pfizer has a product before the FDA allowing aerosolized insulin; I think the FDA will approve it in next couple of years. I think some insurance plans will choose not to cover that. However, if you have a health savings account, you can spend your own money on it.

Unfortunately, in New York, New Jersey, Connecticut, as well as other States, you can't buy a health savings account. I think this bill will allow people with chronic illness, whether it be diabetes or anything else, to pick and choose a State which best matches their needs in terms of regulations and choice of coverage.

Mr. SHADEGG. I yield back my time.

Thank you, Mr. Chairman.

Mr. DEAL. Ms. Baldwin.

Ms. BALDWIN. Thank you, Mr. Chairman. Along with affordability, we need to be absolutely sure that whatever policy a person purchases actually provides coverage to that person when they need it.

We have struggled as a Congress with this issue in a related arena before, with the Patient's Bill of Rights, where a person believes they are fully covered, they faithfully pay their premiums, and when in need, they find their coverage does not provide what they thought they had purchased. But in this arena, we need to make sure that a person who gets diabetes, for example, will have insurance that covers the costs of treatment, counseling, testing materials, as Mr. Limbaugh testified.

We need to make sure that after a person has a heart attack, the insurer doesn't deny benefits claiming that such a person should have known they were going to have a heart attack. We need to make sure that a woman of child-bearing age get a policy that allows her to receive maternity care if and when she needs it. And we need to make insurance affordable for all, not just the young and healthy person who thinks that they are invincible.

All of these are just a few examples of mandates and State laws that protect people with the policies that they buy. And health insurance is not something that the average person, especially one in the individual market, can negotiate.

A State should be able to protect their citizens without being undermined by a lack of regulations in other States. I cited this in my opening statement, that a Commonwealth Fund study earlier this month found there are already 16 million adults who were underinsured in the year 2003; and we don't want to make this problem any bigger.

Mr. Kreidler, can you talk to us a little bit about the dangers of underinsurance for the person buying the insurance and for other individuals in the State?

Mr. KREIDLER. Thank you for that question.

The real dangers with underinsurance—in fact, it is true for the people that are uninsured—is that you wind up with significant cost shifting that takes place in the overall system. That cost is picked up by the other ratepayers; it is built into our rates. That is why it is incredibly important to have more and more people insured. And, in fact, universal coverage would be preferable, rather than having individuals outside the system and coming into the system when they have health needs.

But a real problem exists if you buy an insurance policy that meets your needs from the standpoint you had some special needs, that you are more at risk, and the healthier and younger wind up going over and buying a policy that doesn't have that coverage. When you go to this policy, you find it cost prohibitive and you don't buy it. That means more of it is shifted to you and me because of cost shifting that happens in the system that we have built into our rates and it has the adverse effect of actually driving up the number of uninsured.

Ms. BALDWIN. Thank you.

When most people think about individuals who can't get health insurance because they are sick, they think about individuals with catastrophic illnesses like cancer or AIDS or multiple sclerosis; however, in fact, I think individuals with diabetes also face difficulties in accessing coverage in some States. And I am wondering, Mr. Limbaugh, could you please comment on that? Is it true that individuals with diabetes have difficulty getting insurance because of their medical condition?

Mr. LIMBAUGH. Yes, ma'am, it certainly is true. And it is certainly more true in the four States that have not adopted the diabetes mandates that I spoke of earlier.

I wanted to clarify something, if I could.

I certainly—if I did suggest, I certainly didn't mean to suggest at any point in my testimony that diabetes insurance coverage was not expensive. In fact, it is expensive. Our concern is that it will be even more expensive, if this bill passes and people migrate away from the pools that now include the people with diabetes, that the costs will be even higher.

But, yes, it is difficult in many instances for people with diabetes to find adequate insurance. And I cannot stress strongly enough how crucial it is that the insurance be adequate for people with diabetes, that it cover the tools that they need to manage their disease.

And it is to their benefit, it is to society's benefit, it is to the benefit of the pool of people that have insurance in that program because if you don't manage your disease, the costs are astronomical down the road.

Ms. BALDWIN. Thank you.

Mr. DEAL. Thank you.

Chairman Barton.

Chairman BARTON. Thank you, Mr. Chairman, I want to give everybody a little tidbit of Texas history before we get to the questions. On this day in 1918, the Texas senate passed the 19th amendment, which gave the women of Texas the right to vote. We became the first southern State to do that; and my grandmother—who was not yet my grandmother; she was still unmarried—and her sister, my great aunt, were school teachers in Bosque County, Texas, at Spring Creek, and they promptly went out and registered to vote. And in the next election they voted in the Democrat primary and they voted straight Democrat on the national level.

Of course, there was no Republican Party in Bosque County in 1920, so that kind of begs the question.

A little bit of history. I am going to give you all a little bit of Texas history every now and then.

I want to ask Mr. Kreidler a question. Mr. Shadegg's bill does not remove State regulation. So all the State insurance commissioners would still have the right to enforce regulation of the policies, but it would allow a policy that what was issued in another State to be sold across State lines and it would give the consumers of the States the right to choose what the best policy is for them.

What part of that is bad? What is wrong with, in your home State of Washington, if a Texas insurance company wants to sell a policy, and it is licensed in Texas and it has all the mandates that Texas has—Mr. Matthews says there are 38—what is wrong with giving people of Washington a choice between a Washington-based insurance policy and a Texas-based insurance policy?

Mr. KREIDLER. Thank you, Mr. Chairman.

Let me say that there really are two major issues that are at risk here. No. 1 is that if a consumer has a problem, we have to tell them in my State, if it is a company that they—it is licensed in another State and so it is authorized by that State, licensed in that State, not my State, they are in a position where they are going to have to call—and hopefully it is a 1-800 number—and hope that that State has the resources to address the needs of a non-State resident with problems associated with that.

Chairman BARTON. If Barton Insurance Company in Arlington, Texas, sells a policy to former Congressman John Miller in Spokane, Washington, and former Congressman Miller files a claim with Barton Insurance and Barton Insurance doesn't honor the claim, and it is should be covered, you have the right as Insurance

Commissioner to either, A, cause Barton Insurance to pay the claim, or B, prevent Barton Insurance from issuing any further insurance, don't you?

Mr. KREIDLER. I do have the authority to take them to court and get an injunction against that particular insurer. But it is a far cry from the standpoint of a consumer who has a complaint. There is often a back-and-forth—you haven't paid this bill, whether you submitted it right, resubmit the bill, you didn't check the right boxes, we don't—we are not in a position——

Chairman BARTON. You have staff. As I understand the Shadegg bill, the only thing you can't do is say, before you sell in Washington State, you have to cover everything that our State law says you have to cover. And I understand—I listened to Ms. Baldwin and Ms. Eshoo and Mr. Brown, and I understand the willing—the need to cover as many conditions as we can.

But, you know, markets are about giving people choices; and as long as the two products are portrayed honestly and you are there to make sure that whatever they say they are going to cover, they do cover, why can't a consumer make an honest choice? Why should a consumer have to take, in the most extreme case of Minnesota or New Jersey, policies that cover everything under the sun, that they simply can't afford, so they have no choice, so they have no insurance.

Mr. KREIDLER. Mr. Barton, because we are specifically preempted in being able to do that representation for that consumer who has bought a product licensed in another State, we do not have the ability to do what you are saying.

Chairman BARTON. You have the ability to enforce the policy, unless I misunderstand.

Mr. SHADEGG. Would the gentleman yield?

With all due respect, Mr. Kreidler, you are just simply wrong and you need to more carefully read the bill. You can, in fact, require compliance with all of your State's fraud and abuse laws, and you can require compliance with all of your State's unfair claims and settlement practice laws; all of those are granted to you.

There is a whole list of other things that I have been over before. You can—as you already referred to, you can require compliance with any lawful order, and you can seek an injunction.

So there is a whole list of consumer protections. You may be reading the bill which was introduced last year which was dramatically fewer than these, but these are, in fact, the bill.

Chairman BARTON. My time has expired, but I would really be interested from the insurance commissioner's suggestions about how to strengthen the enforcement section of compliance. I am very interested in that.

I think Mr. Shadegg has a great idea, that we let insurance be sold across State lines; that is going to provide consumers a lot more choice. Having said that, we don't want to let a lot of fly bynight insurance companies come into existence that nobody oversees, so that you pay for the policy, but you don't get any coverage at all.

Mr. SHADEGG. Will the gentleman yield?

In my discussions with the NAIC a week ago, after we had filed the bill, one discussion was this issue of their ability to revoke the license of an insurance company engaged in improper conduct.

What we did discuss with them and have not yet put in the bill is the issue of specifically allowing them to prohibit the sales of the policy; that is to say, if they find any violation of any of their laws that cover this policy or any law of the primary State that covers the policy, to issue an order stopping the sales, which would be similar to revoking licensure. And it is something that would go along the lines of what you were discussing.

Chairman BARTON. I thank the chairman for letting me go over my time.

Mr. DEAL. Mr. Kreidler, I would ask as a follow-up to that, if— from the Association of Commissioners viewpoint if they would review the changes that have been made to the bill and make recommendations of any other tightening or changes that you all would suggest in that regard.

Mr. KREIDLER. Thank you, Mr. Chairman, we are always pleased to work with the members.

Mr. DEAL. Ms. Eshoo.

Ms. ESHOO. Thank you, Mr. Chairman.

One of the arguments that we are hearing today, and I think this is a healthy debate, because there is a recognition of some of the pitfalls. And I think I just heard Mr. Shadegg say that he is considering adding some things to the bill to address them if, in fact, they exist. And I think some of them do.

One of the arguments that we are hearing today is that consumers want bare bones policies, that some insurance is better than none. That is one of the things that I think I am hearing. You know, it sounds plausible until you start looking at some of the statistics nationally, that there are more people that are bankrupted, who are insured, because they are not covered properly with their policies.

Now, I don't know, maybe we need to examine coming up with another tier of insurance in the country nationally; and just say that "This is," just up front, "the cheapest policy that anyone can buy; and this is the minimum amount of coverage"; and that you advertise it that way. And, you know, buyer knows and buyer beware. And that is a form of competition. Because it seems to me that there are more people that want policies that really have embedded them—embedded in them a higher degree of coverage.

For all the reasons that we have the various advocates that we have at the table, that the chairman has seen fit to include in this debate; so anyone that wants to comment on that—I mean, I would welcome your comments.

You know, the idea, the last of the gentlemen to the far right, saying earlier that we have kind of overconsumered things; well, that sounds fine in general until it comes to you specifically. Consumers are not some massive gel. It is each one of us, and the standards that we have in our country.

But I do think the whole notion of those that are not able to buy insurance—you used the example of your daughter, Mr. Chairman—that is something that we need to grapple with; and if that can be done fairly and squarely across the country, I am open to that. But I don't think we should confuse one with the other. I really think there are two distinct issues here.

So who would like to comment on that? Mike?

Mr. KREIDLER. Thank you for the question. And I think one of the real concerns is, because it has been stated that, you know, we have to do something for the younger and healthier person in making sure that they have health insurance. The problem, of course, is what if they get sick? What if they get married and have a baby, and maternity isn't covered, or an illness.

Ms. ESHOO. That is what I said, a real bare bones policy, whatever that policy is that makes it really eminently affordable, but that is not advertised as something that is more than it really is. Is that possible in this country?

Is it possible to offer—I mean, I think it is possible. I think anything is possible. We are America. We are Americans.

Mr. KREIDLER. We want to make sure it has benefit and that you are buying insurance that isn't insurance in name only; and you want to make sure that it has real coverage that is associated with it.

Unfortunately, what is frequently talked about is that the bare bones would not cover diabetes. It would not cover maternity. It would not cover preexisting conditions. And as a result of that, you wind up with certainly something that is very cheap, but would it ever meet your needs?

And that is the concern.

Mr. MATTHEWS. Let me address the Representative's comments.

Some States have passed legislation to create, in essence, bare bones policies.

Ms. ESHOO. How many?

Mr. MATTHEWS. A handful of them, I believe. The interesting thing is, very few people have chosen the bare bones policies. And that goes to your point as to whether or not we ought to create this policy because that is what people want.

I don't think most people want a bare bones policy. Most people want good, adequate coverage, but they want to be able to cover most of the traditional medical problems that they might have. And my understanding, I am not aware of any insurance company that doesn't cover diabetes. There are things within diabetic care like self-management and some of those things that the States have passed laws for—some diabetic supplies. But traditional health insurance is going to cover diabetes.

What we are talking about is people in the individual market; and those people have to generally pay that policy out of their own pocket, and they make tradeoffs.

Most of us would like to have the most benefits we can, but we ask, How much can we afford, given the fact that we are buying the policy, and how much are we going to be able to get included in that.

What most people in the individual market do right now is they will move to a higher deductible $2,000-$2,500 deductible, but then they have full coverage above that, because that becomes a much more affordable policy. And I expect you would find people moving to variations of that, and different types innovative policies, but I would be very surprised if you find a lot of people moving to what we call a "bare bones policy." They are available now and a lot of people just don't want them.

Ms. ESHOO. I think we need more data on that, Mr. Chairman, on this issue of the bare bones policy, what States offer, what that policy actually covers, so that we know what is in play out there. Because one is not going to substitute for the other in my mind.

But I appreciate this. I think it has been a worthwhile—more than a worthwhile hearing.

Mr. DEAL. Thank the gentlelady.

Dr. Norwood.

Mr. NORWOOD. Thank you, Mr. Chairman.

Mrs. Eshoo, I agree with you. Ms. Eshoo, ma'am, I agree with you.

Ms. Eshoo, I agree with you on the basic health care policy. I am not sure that means bare bones; bare bones and basic aren't necessarily the same thing. But I do hope we—I have thought about that a lot. I just can't imagine getting any 10 people in the world in the room to agree on a basic policy. But there is a place for that.

Mr. Matthews, let me ask you a couple of questions.

Do the State legislators in your research and in your work evaluate the cost of each and every mandate before they implement it? Do you know the answer to that.

Mr. MATTHEWS. It is a good question.

Many States have moved to legislation that requires them to evaluate the cost of a health insurance mandate before they implement it—in some cases, if my recollection serves me correctly, even requiring the State employees to have it for a certain amount of time before, to evaluate the cost of it. So some States are moving in that direction simply because they are finding out that the mandates had been passing.

Mr. NORWOOD. Are they looking at the cumulative effect? Do Texas and Georgia look at all 38 mandates and determine, hey, this is costing X amount on a premium? Are people thinking that out?

Mr. MATTHEWS. You have some State legislators who do, but typically no.

What they are looking at is the cost of each individual mandate, and then the debate is over whether or not this mandate actually costs people more or saves more. And I can guarantee you there is not one special interest group out there—and I don't mean that in a pejorative sense—that doesn't say, if you cover our particular provider, supplies, service, it will lower the health insurance cost.

Mr. NORWOOD. I have got a lot to ask, Mr. Kreidler. How about insurance commissioners, do they think like that the all? What is the cost? What is the cumulative cost of mandates?

Mr. KREIDLER. The answer is, yes, we do think about it. But a lot depends on how you define what mandates are. Is it a mandate, a requirement that the insurer can't take into account preexisting conditions?

Mr. NORRIS. A mandate is when a legislature tells an insurance company, if you want to sell insurance in my State, this has got to be in your policy. That is what a mandate is.

Mr. KREIDLER. And frequently we wind up hearing mandates talked about, whether it is acupuncture, chiropractic and other types of services.

Mr. NORWOOD. Nobody is saying they are all bad. A lot of people are saying there are a lot of bad ones in there.

Mr. Limbaugh, there are four States—did I understand you to say there are four States that don't have a——

Mr. LIMBAUGH. Yes, sir, diabetes mandate.

Mr. NORWOOD. Diabetes mandate?

Mr. LIMBAUGH. Yes. Yes, sir.

Mr. NORWOOD. Now, my understanding of this bill—and I will direct this to Mr. Shadegg.

Does that mean that the other 44 States, Mr. Shadegg, will still have diabetes mandates when this bill is passed?

Mr. SHADEGG. Will the gentleman yield?

Absolutely, they will still have the mandates and people will still be able to buy the policy that has those mandated coverages.

Mr. NORWOOD. Do you agree with that, Mr. Limbaugh?

Mr. LIMBAUGH. I agree that, in theory, it is possible that there will be insurance companies that continue to domicile in one of those 46 States. I am not convinced that any right-thinking insurance company wouldn't domicile in the State that has the fewest regulations and mandates and work from there.

Mr. NORWOOD. Well, they do now, they presently are in, you say, 46. Is that correct, 46 States? So my suggestion is, the thing to do is work on these four States that don't have mandates, rather than work on this bill.

Mr. LIMBAUGH. We are working as hard as we can on both, Congressman.

Mr. NORWOOD. Dr. Matthews, are there some critical benefit mandates in your work that you have come across, A, B, and C that are critical?

Mr. MATTHEWS. When you say "critical," I think it is fair to say that insurance companies—there has sort of been the impression that insurance companies are going to not pay for something even if there is a cost/benefit in paying for it.

Insurance companies that are covering individuals want to be able to reduce the cost of the care that those individuals are having to receive. If preventive care, screening and other things help with that, it is much better, it is more cost effective, as has been commented on, for the insurance companies to provide the care on diabetes rather than have various types of hospital incidents.

Mr. NORWOOD. Well, does emergency services—would that be considered a critical mandate, in your mind?

Mr. MATTHEWS. My recollection is most emergency services, when you show up at a hospital and you need care, it is covered by traditional insurance.

Mr. NORWOOD. I am talking about the insurance policy—as a State legislature mandating in that policy that you cover emergency services; is that critical to a policy?

Mr. MATTHEWS. Yes, it would be critical to a policy. I think most insurance companies do it anyway.

Mr. NORWOOD. But some States don't have that mandate.

Mr. MATTHEWS. I am not aware of a person going into an emergency room and not having——

Mr. NORWOOD. No, that is not what I am saying. I am talking about the mandate in the policy.

Pennsylvania, for example, does not mandate that the insurance companies practicing in their State have that mandate. Yet we don't hear that outcry from the State of Pennsylvania that nobody is being taken care of.

My point is that some critical mandates are already being tended to.

Mr. MATTHEWS. That is my point.

Mr. NORWOOD. I yield.

Mr. DEAL. We have agreement on something.

Dr. Burgess, you are recognized for 8 minutes.

Mr. BURGESS. Thank you. Thank you, Mr. Chairman.

Mr. Kreidler, there are, I have been a big believer in MSAs and HSAs for a long time. And I think that HSAs have shown a good deal of promise in helping people who are uninsured.

The chairman alluded to his daughter. Ten years ago, my daughter, in a similar situation, same age, 25, elected not to work and decided she didn't need health insurance; and I could not purchase a policy. At the time, I was a practicing physician willing to write a big check to get her health insurance, and I couldn't find it. No one would sell it to me at any cost.

Now a 25-year-old can go on the Internet, type in "health savings accounts" and suddenly there is a panoply of insurance policies available to them that are very affordable with a high deductible. But on the concept of HSAs, one insurer has reported that 18 percent, in electing an HSA, were previously uninsured, which is a pretty powerful piece of information if we are truly concerned about bringing down the number of uninsured.

But HSAs are not available in all 50 of the States. Do you know why that is?

Mr. KREIDLER. No, I couldn't explain why other States don't.

But let me say that HSAs, I think, are a reasonable product, as long as you wind up having the kind of major medical, that you have that kind of backup to it, so that you can guarantee that when you go past a certain threshold you are going to have coverage, so you have a major medical backing it up. If you do that, that works well.

I think the challenge that we face is, too many people wind up, when they are healthy and younger, saying they want an HSA. If they develop some kind of chronic disease or when they get a little older, they are less inclined to want to make that investment, particularly if they are less well at that point. It is trying to find the balance of making sure that the people that are in there can cover the costs.

And insurance companies have clearly found that it sometimes is very expensive in offering that package to an individual because they are getting people when they are younger and healthier, and they are keeping the money as opposed to the others that wind up then having more costs, opting out and going toward the broader coverage.

Mr. BURGESS. The brief period of time when I had an MSA, which is when they were first allowed by Chairman Archer in 1997, up until the time I came to Congress in 2003, a significant amount of cash accrued in that policy. And if there is one thing that I took away from that lesson was, it is possible for a person to put away money for their medical care for future needs. And even though I am covered under one of the plans here in the House now, and we don't have it now, unfortunately, an HSA available to us in the House; that money still sits there and grows year over year with simple compound interest; and that will basically be my prescription drug plan when I go on Medicare.

Dr. Gratzer, did you have something you want to say about that?

Mr. GRATZER. I just want to add to your point. There was an article in the Wall Street Journal, written by Susan Locke 2 days ago—I believe she won a Pulitzer prize on health reporting—and she was talking about this issue of health savings accounts being this new innovative policy passed by Congress as part of the Medicare Modernization Act, very attractive to young people—unless you happen to live in a State like New York, New Jersey or Connecticut where the regulatory malaise is so bad you can't get a policy.

One of the great things about this act isn't just the cost savings to young people, which a lot of people have talked about and I talked about in my original statement, that effectively these mandates are a hidden tax—as all regulations, I suppose, are—but what you find in States like New York is that the competitive market for health insurance doesn't exist.

I hope, if you are a New Yorker, you like managed care because if you are in the individual market, your choices are managed care, managed care, or managed care; you can't get a health savings account. And I think that really speaks to the fact that there has been regulatory overdrive in many States, and a competitive market means that you ought to be allowed to go to New York and, if you are a New Yorker, buy a managed care package for a whole lot of money; but you also ought to have the right to buy out of State, the way you buy out of State in terms of banking and mortgages. And I think health savings accounts are part of the solution.

Let's not overstate it. They are not going to solve all the problems of American health care. What a great step in the right direction. Let's make sure it applies to people in all the States.

Mr. BURGESS. I couldn't agree more, Dr. Matthews.

On the concept of the race to the bottom that people will short themselves on health care, I think NCPA in Dallas several years ago did a study on just that one issue with MSAs, looking at pharmaceuticals what might be considered lifestyle drugs—Ritalin, and the actual utilization of Ritalin went down among people who were using a MSA;whereas another drug, such as Fosomax that would prevent osteoporosis, the utilization went up. That is, people were willing to invest in their care for the long term if it was in their best interest.

Have I accurately summarized that?

Mr. MATTHEWS. You have. And the broader point of what you are suggesting is, we are moving into an age in which we are leaving a doctor-directed health care system to more of a patient-directed health care system, where patients have more access to information, more—they are more concerned about this. It is a growing consumer market in health care. We can't stop that.

Mr. BURGESS. Mr. Limbaugh, do you have any evidence that would suggest that programs like disease management in diabetics would fall by the wayside if Mr. Shadegg's legislation were to pass? You made the point, talking about diabetes—of course, no differentiation between Type 1 and Type 2 diabetes—where, in fact, there are some lifestyle changes that they could encourage in people who will develop maturity-onset or adult-onset diabetes.

I think, Dr. Zerhouni, when he was here, was talking about that—from the National Institutes of Health—said that if he could convince people to lose 5 to 7 pounds, we would save just a ton of money in this country as far as the management of diabetes. And obviously that is not a savings that we want to walk away from, but you seem to have some concern that if this type of program were to become law that that activity would fall by the wayside; and I wondered if you have any evidence to that effect.

Mr. LIMBAUGH. Well, I don't have any evidence of what—I don't have any evidence of what the future is going to bring. I mean, what I do know is, in the 46 States that have made the decision to mandate diabetes coverage for people who manage their disease, that not one of the States has ever repealed the mandate. Some States have strengthened it after they passed it.

And my concern is—as I have said, is that the mandates that we have adopted in those 46 States will be threatened by this legislation because an insurer can domicile in another State that doesn't have the mandates, and they won't be available.

And it seems—it seems to me that these mandates were adopted for a good reason, a good public policy reason.

In my real life, I do government relations in eight States in the South, and I have never been in a State capital where the diabetes lobby was stronger than the business and health care insurance lobby.

Mr. BURGESS. My time is up. I think Dr. Gratzer had something he wanted to say, to add to that. Did I interpret that correctly?

Mr. GRATZER. No.

Mr. BURGESS. I would say to some extent we have that now. I know, from my life as a private physician, I know plenty of times I was on the phone from 1-800 Minneapolis to try to get my surgery approved or my patient's medication approved. We have that now. For the life of me, I didn't see that that was necessarily helpful in my daily practice of medicine. I will yield back.

Mr. DEAL. Out of curiosity, will you tell us who the four States are who don't mandate it?

Mr. LIMBAUGH. It is Ohio, Alabama, Idaho and North Dakota.

Mr. DEAL. Nobody is going to locate an insurance company in those States anyway. We will recognize Mr. Waxman real quickly, because we are on a vote. We will back after the vote.

Mr. Waxman.

Mr. WAXMAN. Thank you, Mr. Chairman.

Mr. Kreidler, good to see you in our committee. You should be up here, in my view. I have heard it said in order to bring health insurance into the 21st Century we need to enact this legislation under discussion today.

Supposedly, you could buy anything anywhere on the Internet free from State regulation, and I would like to understand if this is true. Mr. Kreidler, can a person living in one State buy disability insurance from an insurer regulated in another State to get a cheaper policy?

Mr. KREIDLER. No, they cannot.

Mr. WAXMAN. Can a person in one State buy life insurance from an insurer regulated in another State to get a cheaper policy?

Mr. KREIDLER. No, they cannot.

Mr. WAXMAN. Can one person living in one State buy homeowners insurance from an insurer regulated in another State to get a cheaper policy?

Mr. KREIDLER. Only if they are licensed in the domestic State, in the State in which it is issued.

Mr. WAXMAN. Can a person living in one State buy auto insurance regulated in another State?

Mr. KREIDLER. No.

Mr. WAXMAN. So health insurance isn't the only insurance which must be regulated in the State in which it is purchased. Would you say that the law requires almost all insurance to be regulated by the State in which it is purchased?

Mr. KREIDLER. That is correct.

Mr. WAXMAN. Are there any exceptions to this rule?

Mr. KREIDLER. Yes, risk retention groups and surplus lines like Lloyd's of London where you are buying the very high cost that is not backed up by guarantee fund?

Mr. WAXMAN. What recourse do individuals in the group have if these types of insurance go under?

Mr. KREIDLER. If they are licensed in another State, if they are licensed in a State where the policy was issued, they clearly have the authority of the regulator to keep—whether they keep their license or not, can bring an injunction against them, a cease and desist order. We do market conduct examinations. We are able to intervene on behalf of the affected consumer effectively.

Mr. WAXMAN. That is somebody in the same State.

Mr. KREIDLER. Same State.

Mr. WAXMAN. Do you believe it would be wise to change the way health insurance is regulated so it is more like the risk retention groups?

Mr. KREIDLER. No, I would clearly not. I would think it would be a huge mistake.

Mr. WAXMAN. Do you believe that consumers would be at risk if carriers were allowed to choose which State it would be regulated in and then sell products internationally?

Mr. KREIDLER. Very definitely.

Mr. WAXMAN. Proponents of this legislation believe it will lower health care costs through competition, but I don't believe there is much evidence that the number of carriers, licensed carriers in a State affects costs. Today, there are 53 licensed health insurers in Montana versus 54 in New Jersey. This is according to the American Health Insurance Plan's website.

All States have tons of licensed carriers, most of which sell only a tiny bit of coverage. In every State, three carriers comprise 50 to 100 percent of the market share, and half of all carriers comprise 4 to 8 percent of the market share. Most insurers compete on the basis of cherry picking, and you can only do that well if you have a small number of enrollees to keep track of.

Additionally, studies show that the increasing cost of health care in our Nation is not because of growing State mandates in regulations. The cost drivers are in-patient hospital care, prescription drug costs, growth and spending on physician services. In-patient hospital costs accounted for 54 percent of the increase in health care spending in 2004. Prescription drugs counted for 21 percent. Physician services accounted for 24 percent of the increase in health care spending in 2004, according to the Center for Studying Health System Change.

Mr. Kreidler, do you believe that we will magically lower health care costs by any significant amount by enacting this legislation?

Mr. KREIDLER. No, we will not.

Mr. WAXMAN. How would a single State be able to monitor and regulate the sale of insurance across all 50 States. Do you, for example, in your budget, have enough money to assist consumers in other States if a plan licensed in your State was causing problems for them elsewhere?

Mr. KREIDLER. Mr. Waxman, we received literally thousands of inquiries on a monthly basis. We do those for people that reside in our State. If, in fact, we are receiving those inquiries from the rest of the country, clearly we would not. Our first priority would be in-state at the expense of those out-of-state.

Mr. WAXMAN. I would like to follow up on something Mr. de Posada said. A person in Washington State that wants the option of buying a cheaper policy from another State will not necessarily be able to get that same policy for the same cheap price, because the costs of providing the services in Washington State would be more expensive than the service costs in another State. Is that true?

Mr. KREIDLER. No, it is not.

Mr. WAXMAN. So, you disagree.

One last question in the 10 seconds I have. Wouldn't we end up with more sham plans on the marketplace and more consumers in trouble? For example, the experience with municipal welfare agencies or MWAs as they are often called is that the Department of Labor couldn't monitor the sale across the whole country. How can a State insurance department with even less staff adequately monitor what is going on, Mr. Kreidler?

Mr. KREIDLER. You are clearly right, Mr. Waxman. It would present a challenge that could not be matched by a State that had little or no regulation. They typically have little or no staff. They would not be able to do the kind of monitoring that is required.

Mr. WAXMAN. Thank you.

Thank you, Mr. Chairman.

Mr. DEAL. Mr. de Posada, would you like to respond?

Mr. DE POSADA. Yes, I actually checked. I am uninsured. I was trying to purchase an HSA in Washington State. I compared it to Virginia. I would actually have to pay three times more in Washington State than I would in Virginia. Clearly, there is a price differential right now.

The only thing I have right now is American Express travel insurance for emergencies when I am outside of Washington State. So there are substantial price benefits.

Mr. DEAL. The committee is going to stand in recess until after these votes. I think there are only two. We did have some members who had questions who have left, but they will be back, I think.

So we are in recess. If you will stay with us, we will stand in recess temporarily.

[Brief recess.]

Mr. DEAL. We will reconvene the hearing. Apparently, the absence has dissipated those who had questions otherwise from returning, unless Mr. Shimkus has questions, do you have questions, Mr. Shimkus?

Mr. SHIMKUS. Is that yes? What do you want, Mr. Chairman?

Mr. DEAL. You are an agent of your own free will in this hearing.

Mr. SHIMKUS. All right. Thank you. Not a question, Mr. Chair, just a short statement.

Mr. DEAL. All right.

Mr. SHIMKUS. I apologize. Let me just say that I am very excited. I am glad to cosponsor Congressman Shadegg's legislation. I do think the interstate commerce clause in the Gramm-Leach-Bliley Act moves us to this ability for people to choose.

You have got to be able to trust individual consumers, whether it is on the product itself or the services or the protections rendered by an insurance product in a certain State. I think, given those variables, we have a great opportunity to help decrease the number of uninsured. I am a big supporter of the health savings accounts, and I think we need to move forward, Mr. Chairman. My questions were going to be in that line. I will just do a statement.

I yield back.

Mr. DEAL. I thank the gentleman.

Mr. Limbaugh, now that we have all attacked Mr. Brown's home State, he wants to defend it, and I will recognize him to do that.

Mr. BROWN. Mr. Limbaugh, if you have any comments—no, I appreciate you bringing it up. Three years ago, a bunch of us worked with the Diabetes Association, a Republican from Cincinnati, a Republican from my district. I was involved in a lot of work in the legislature.

The insurance industry stopped Ohio from being the 47th, I believe, State at that time. So I am a little embarrassed by it. We should do better. I would imagine that it has an impact in the State that we haven't been able to do it.

Mr. LIMBAUGH. Yes, Congressman Brown, thank you. It certainly does. Our information is that there is something on the order of 750,000 people in Ohio who have diabetes and 100,000 of them who have insurance but don't have diabetes coverage. It is—we are continuing to work in Ohio to try to change that.

We, as I said, we have been successful in 46 States; I tried to say earlier. I think I fumbled it a little bit. I am not aware of any State where the diabetes lobby is stronger than the insurance and business lobby in this country. But notwithstanding that fact, we have been able to convince these legislatures of the importance of having a diabetes mandate.

We will continue to try to convince the legislature in Ohio that we, in fact, have ongoing, as we speak, a very strong push again this year to try to get the Diabetes Cost Reduction Act, which is what we call the mandate, passed in Ohio.

People who don't have adequate coverage, who have insurance but don't have adequate coverage and have diabetes are essentially paying for the privilege of being uninsured, as far as their diabetes goes. A person with diabetes is going to pay something on the order of $200 to $400 a month to manage their disease.

When you are paying an insurance premium and you are not covered for that, it is a pretty aggravating situation, both personally and financially, because you are having to spend a lot of money out of your pocket. You are still not getting the insurance coverage that you need.

Thank you.

Mr. DEAL. Thank you. I am sure Mr. Shadegg would probably add that if the four States get their mandated coverage in place. He would expect your support of his bill; is that right?

Mr. SHADEGG. Absolutely.

Mr. LIMBAUGH. We would suggest, perhaps as a compromise, just including the mandate in the bill.

Mr. DEAL. Well, with that, we will conclude the hearing. Once again, thank all of you. It has been a very informative hearing. We appreciate all of your points of view. There may be some issues that you may wish to submit additional information to us on. We would welcome that. There may be some questions from some of the committee members who would ask you to respond to.

Yes, Michael.

Mr. KREIDLER. Mr. Chairman, I would just like to correct a statement I made relative to the cost of health care insurance in one State being something that would be—and let us say it was cheaper in another State and then cost more in another State. You couldn't—what really drives it are the costs of medical services. So you wouldn't see the price from the cheaper State directly applied.

Mr. DEAL. I think we understood that. I think that is the reason you see Medicare and Medicaid reimbursement is higher in those States because of the cost of providing the care.

Well, thank you all again.

This hearing is adjourned.

[Whereupon, at 12:45 p.m., the subcommittee was adjourned.]

[Additional material submitted for the record follows:]

Post-Hearing Questions
U.S. House of Representatives
Committee on Energy and Commerce
Subcommittee on Health

The Honorable Mike Kreidler, Commissioner of Insurance, State of Washington Representing the National Association of Insurance Commissioners

"H.R. 2355, the Health Care Choice Act"
June 28, 2005

Questions submitted by Rep. John Dingell, Ranking Minority Member of Full Committee:

1. **What are examples of some of the financial solvency laws and processes for enforcing those laws that a State would no longer be able to use on an insurer or product that is licensed in another State and offered to the residents of your State under the proposed "Health Care Choice Act of 2005"? Are there any examples of particularly strong laws in these areas from other States that would be undermined?**

A. H.R. 2355 requires the Primary State to use "risk based capital" standards and to oversee the financial solvency of the insurers it has licensed. The bill also allows the Secondary State to step in should the Primary State fail to perform due diligence in ensuring the financial stability of an insurer operating in the Secondary State.

First, although the bill requires the use of risk-based capital, that term is undefined. Unless there are standards set for risk based capital (e.g. NAIC standards), a state can adopt inadequate RBC standards, thereby vitiating the entire reason for RBC in the first place. A secondary state's higher standards are preempted.

Second, while the provisions attempt to protect consumers, there is still a concern about enforcement. Under current law, if an insurer does not maintain sufficient capital reserves or surpluses the state may call for an audit, take over the financial activities of the company, or even withdraw the license. Under H.R. 2355, the ability of the Secondary State to hold the insurer accountable is questionable. How can the Secondary State perform an audit of an insurer licensed in another state? How can the Secondary State take over the financial activities of a company in another state? How can a Secondary State stop the operations of an insurer without a license in its state?

The limited ability of the Secondary State, under H.R. 2355, to protect its citizens from an insurer it has not licensed is one of the primary concerns of the NAIC.

2. What information is necessary for a State to assess premiums and other taxes on policies offered in that State? Does the "Health Care Choice Act of 2005" require insurers to provide such information to the appropriate entities in the secondary State where the insurer is offering products but the product is licensed in another primary State?

A. The Secondary State must have access to the amount of premium collected by the insurer from beneficiaries in the Secondary State. This information is available from the annual statements filed by all insurers with the Primary State and the NAIC. Each annual statement has "State Pages" that include the amount of premium collected by the insurer in each state in which it operates. Theoretically, H.R. 2355 would not limit the ability of the Secondary State to collect this information or the premium taxes. However, it is important to remember that the company is unlicensed in the Secondary State, and in the case of a recalcitrant actor, actual collection of the funds could be more complicated than when dealing with a licensed company.

3. What information is necessary for an insurer to participate in an insurance insolvency guaranty association or similar association in a State? Does the "Health Care Choice Act of 2005" require insurers to provide such information to the appropriate entities in the secondary State where the insurer is offering products but the product is licensed in another primary State?

A. See answer to question #2. The annual statement includes sufficient information for the Secondary State to collect necessary taxes, fees and assessments for guaranty funds. However, the same warning applies to actual collection of the funds.

4. To what extent does the "Health Care Choice Act of 2005" open the door to fraudulent activity? This bill merely requires insurers to self-attest to the secondary States in which they want to offer policies that they are complying with all the requirements of the primary State. The primary State does not have to corroborate this self-certification nor respond to inquiries from a secondary State about an insurer. Are you concerned by the lack of a requirement for the primary State to verify that an insurer is indeed licensed and in good standing to offer that same product in a secondary State?

A. There is no doubt in the minds of the nation's insurance regulators that H.R. 2355 would result in increased fraud. The number one claim of fraudulent plans is that they are not subject to state regulation. They claim to be an ERISA plan, or a Multiple Employer Welfare Arrangement or a union plan that is exempt from state law. Once these unlicensed plans are discovered, it often takes months to prove that they are not exempt, and by that time millions of dollars in premiums are gone.

H.R. 2355 would create another vehicle by which fraudulent plans could claim exemption from state law – opening the door to more unscrupulous operators.

PREPARED STATEMENT OF DEBRA L. NESS, PRESIDENT, NATIONAL PARTNERSHIP FOR WOMEN & FAMILIES

NATIONAL HEALTH CARE ADVOCATE OPPOSES THE HEALTH CARE CHOICE ACT

Women need access to high quality, affordable health care for themselves and their families. We must consider a range of different options to resolve the health care crisis, but the Health Care Choice Act, H.R. 2355, is not the answer. We hope that today's hearing will reveal the deep flaws of the proposal and lead to consideration of real solutions to help Americans deal with the rising cost of health care coverage.

The Health Care Choice Act would allow insurers offering individual health insurance plans to choose one state and its rules to regulate plans sold in all states. Insurers could select the state with the most lenient rules, and thereby circumvent state laws that protect consumers from unfair rates and rate hikes. These insurers would be exempt from other critical consumer protections such as guaranteed coverage for individuals with preexisting conditions, and required coverage of critical health benefits like mammography screenings and preventive care. Insurers could also avoid HIPAA-guaranteed access protections for those losing group coverage and moving into the individual market.

In addition to the loss of consumer protections, there would be no effective enforcement mechanism to protect consumers against abuses by insurance companies and assist them with remedies. Today, individuals seek recourse through their own state's insurance commissioner, who regulates the policies they purchase. Under this bill, their state insurance commissioner will have no jurisdiction or ability to enforce rules for a policy issued through another state, leaving a regulatory vacuum for consumers.

The National Partnership urges members of the Subcommittee to reject this proposal that would harm people in the already volatile individual market. The Subcommittee should consider real solutions to expand access to affordable and comprehensive coverage, help those most in need, provide strong consumer protections and offer meaningful solutions for covering the uninsured.

The National Partnership for Women & Families is a nonprofit, nonpartisan organization that uses public education and advocacy to promote fairness in the workplace, quality health care, and policies that help women and men meet the dual demands of work and family.

○

APEX
TP
9780160740008
76901953-8